CW00591264

GETTING SALES

GETTING SALES

Richard D Smith
and
Ginger Dick

Kogan
Page

Kogan Page acknowledge the assistance of Ian Linton
in the preparation of this edition.

First published in Canada in 1981 by International Self-Counsel
Press Ltd, North Vancouver, British Columbia
Copyright © Richard D Smith & Associates 1981

This edition, with additional material, first published in
Great Britain in 1984 by Kogan Page Ltd, 120 Pentonville Road
London N1 9JN
Additional material copyright © Kogan Page Ltd 1984

British Library Cataloguing in Publication Data

Smith, Richard D.
   Getting sales.
   1. Selling
   I. Title   II. Dick, Ginger
   658.8'5   HF5438.25
   ISBN 0-85038-712-4
   ISBN 0-85038-713-2 Pbk

Printed by Billing & Sons Limited, Worcester.

Contents

What This Book Will Do For You   9

Introduction   11

1. Matching Your Product to the Market   13

What are you really selling? 13; What is a benefit? 14;
What is a selling point? 15; Which of these 10 buying motives
could you sell to? 16; Who will need and buy what you sell? 20;
How you can find out when people will buy from you 20;
How businesses can use selling cycles 21; Use competitive analysis
to uncover more benefits 25; Positioning makes you number
one 26; How to use your success analysis worksheets 28;
Success analysis worksheets 29; Benefits/Buying motives 30;
Product/Service life cycle and timing analysis 31; Competitive
situation analysis 32; Selling points and features analysis 34;
Portrait of your product, service or shop 35

2. Enlarging Your Customer Base   36

Three sources of increased sales 36; Four things customers or
prospects should always be told 37; Techniques for selling more
to current customers 37; Let current customers lead you to new
ones 38; Leads and referrals — your business lifeblood 39;
30 Local sources of new customer groups 44; Keeping your
lists up to date 47, Worksheet for building a customer base for
increased sales 48

3. Techniques for Face-to-Face and Telephone Selling   50

10 Most common reasons why a prospect does not buy 50;
10 Ways to tell if a prospect is ready to buy 51; The six steps to
building a sale 54; 10 Direct selling techniques that work 57;
Using your telephone to get sales 59; Effective prospecting
calls 60; Using a telephone script 67, 10 Tips for more effective
telephone use 67; Personal and telephone selling worksheet 71

4. Using Free Publicity, Local Community Groups and Public Relations to Make Yourself Known 73

73

How local community groups and customer/public relations can help you sell 74; 25 Ways to use community service public relations to build sales 74; How to get free publicity for your business 80; Writing good press releases 81; Two publicity success stories 84; Sample press release 86

5. Using Sales Promotion and Direct Mail to Build Your Business

87

What is sales promotion? 87; How to organise a sales promotion 88; Promotion planning checklist 91; Ideas for sales promotions 93; How to use a demonstration for promotion 101; How to use displays to build sales 105; Worksheet for demonstration or seminar ideas 107; What is direct mail? 107; Measuring the results of all promotions 110; Six-week report on mailing piece results 198X 111

6. Using Advertising Effectively

113

Choosing and scheduling your media cost — effectively 113; Media evaluation/costing worksheet 118; Finding local advertising and promotion specialists 120; Advertising that stands out and sells 123; Copy and layout checklist for print advertising 125

7. Coop Advertising Saves Money

127

What is coop advertising? 127; Using coop advertising effectively 131; Other coop opportunities 132; Coop materials checklist 134; Coop record keeping with manufacturers 135; Coop advertising record 136; Building cash flow 137; Getting the best out of your coop materials 138

8. Managing Your Selling Time Effectively

139

30 Time wasters that cost you sales 139; Time/Cost management for consultants and personal service business 148; Two common time traps 151; Time management analysis worksheet 153

9. Evaluating Your Sales Success

154

Review your plan regularly 154; 12 Ways to evaluate your sales success 154; Sales success analysis worksheet 157

Additional Sources of Information

Useful addresses 158; Further reading 160

What This Book Will Do For You

The purpose of this book is to help you get more sales for your business. If you have not yet started your own business, you will find suggestions for pinpointing and selling to those customer groups who would most benefit from your product or service. If you have already established a business, you will learn the selling tools and techniques to increase your sales to both current and new customer groups. Throughout this book, you will find more than 200 proven ideas and suggestions to increase your sales, often illustrated by detailed case histories that show you how to use these tools in your own business.

Although this book aims to provide accurate and authoritative information on the subject matter covered, it is sold on the understanding that neither the authors nor the publisher are rendering legal, accounting or other professional advice. If legal advice or other expert assistance is required, the services of a competent local professional should be sought.

Introduction

A sale is one of the most human of all transactions. It involves thinking, feeling, imagination, and service, as well as an exchange of money for goods and services.

Before exploring the specific techniques of getting more sales, take a moment here to review the elements that make a sale satisfactory for both buyer and seller. A brief analysis of these four main elements will show why they are so important in building your business over the long term. Each satisfactory sale should include:

An agreement. This is the simplest and most visible level of a sale, yet the one most often abused. Your agreement as the seller is to provide your customers or clients with products or services of at least equal value to the money they will give you in exchange. The real value involved is in the *benefits* your customer gets from your product or service. In what ways does your product improve, simplify, beautify, or add something to the customer's business or personal life? (The sections on product analysis and advertising will show you how to determine and sell benefits.) Success at this level means ensuring that what you sell provides honest value for money. This makes the buyer happy, and leads to the next element you want in all your sales.

Trust. All sales agreements should be based on trust and respect between buyer and seller. If a sale is appropriate to your customer's wants, needs, and ability to pay, that sale will lead to satisfaction. If not, the buyer will leave with a feeling of being taken advantage of or 'conned'. It is your responsibility as the seller to get the kind of information from customers that will lead to appropriate sales and build trust. You don't need to sell to those who cannot afford or will not get value from your offering. In fact, sales that are not to the mutual advantage of buyer and seller will hinder the development of the next important element — repeat business.

An interdependent relationship. A good sale should be

the beginning of a long-term relationship, in which buyer and seller continue to serve each other's business needs. You want each sale (or contract) to build loyalty to you and your business, so that your customers keep coming back to you.

The higher the price or value of each purchase, the more personal (in the business sense) this long-term relationship with your customers will be. Whatever your business, one of your long-range sales goals should be to build up and maintain a core of steady repeat customers or clients. Suggestions for building repeat business are included in the sections on customer groups and on selling tools and techniques.

A real or perceived benefit or service that fills a customer need or desire. Though mentioned briefly in point one, this element of the sale is so critical to your sales success that it cannot be over-emphasised. If there is no need or desire for what you are offering, you won't be in business for long. If you cannot convey the benefits of your offering to the people who would appreciate and value them, you won't have the sales.

The best way to market a product or service is to find a need in the market place that you can fill, then 'fit' your product or service to that need. Do the worksheet on customer buying motives in the product analysis section to evaluate where your offering would fit into the customer's spending patterns and how you could best sell into customer needs.

You and/or your staff must also remain sensitive to how the customer expresses real or perceived needs during the course of a sales transaction. This important process is explored more fully in the sections on face-to-face and telephone selling techniques. The desire to serve customers well in every sale is the hallmark of the seller with integrity. If your product or service gives value, fills a customer's want or need, and lives up to customer expectations, the tools and techniques in this book will help you increase your sales significantly. If not, take heed from David Ogilvy, the advertising wizard, who once said, 'Nothing kills a mediocre product more quickly than to make people aware of it.'

The results you achieve from this book will be directly proportionate to the amount of thought and effort you put into *using* it. Do the exercises and worksheets, as well as reading the tips and techniques. Pick out and adapt those tools and techniques most suitable for your business. Then go out and SELL!

Chapter 1

Matching Your Product to the Market

What are you *really* selling?

Do you know what you're really selling? It probably isn't what you think. You may think you're selling cosmetics, when you're actually selling beauty and sex appeal. If your product is a consulting service, you're selling 'getting the job done'. Are you selling craft or hobby kits? The customer is buying an enjoyable leisure activity that adds beauty and satisfaction to life. With machine tools, you could be selling improved performance, less downtime, or production savings.

In any business, you're actually selling *what your product or service will do for the customer*. The 'reward factors' that customers get when they buy from you are called benefits. Benefits are the reasons why people buy from you.

This chapter is about finding and selling the benefits of your own product or service. You will learn about the 10 basic reasons why customers buy, and you will learn how to fit your benefits into customer needs. You will analyse the competition, and see how you can use the benefits you offer to outsell your rivals. You will also learn about your 'selling cycle', which is your key to repeat sales.

At the end of this chapter, you will find a success analysis worksheet designed to help you focus on what you are selling. Complete the worksheet after you read the chapter. It is a step-by-step guide to your own benefits, selling points, timing, customer buying motives, and competitive strategies that can lead you to sales success.

Even if your business is already established, use this chapter to focus on benefits that would create new selling opportunities for you. Refresh your memory, and generate some new enthusiasm about the tremendous product or service you are selling.

If you are planning or just starting a new business, do the worksheet before you take another step. It is designed to give you the kind of insight you need about your product and your business goals that will help you build sales realistically.

As the starting point in your sales plan, a careful analysis of your product or service benefits is the first logical step.

What is a benefit?

Among dictionary definitions of a benefit are 'an act of kindness; gift; benefaction. Whatever promotes welfare; advantage; profit; specifically monetary advantage or profit'.

In selling, a benefit is anything that promotes the welfare of your customer once the product or service is purchased. The benefit is the *end result* of what your product or service can do for the customer.

Does your product or service offer customers a way to save time or money, enhance their appearance, bring more comfort into their lives, add to their pride or status, impress the neighbours or business colleagues, or in some other way add something desirable to their lives? These are all benefits, and could be considered 'acts of kindness' resulting from your sale.

Successful manufacturers, retailers, and service businesses know how benefits can work to inspire and motivate sales. Look at the advertising you see every day. When car manufacturers talk about 'luxury' or 'economy' or 'more miles per gallon to save you money', they're stressing benefits. When an advertiser tells you you'll get a certain result from owning a product (look younger, feel better, have a more beautiful home, run your business more profitably etc), you are being promised a benefit.

You can see even more clearly how benefits can motivate sales through a simple example from your own life. Think of the last suit or dress you bought. Essentially, a suit or dress is merely a covering for your body and, if covering were all you wanted, a sheet would have done the job as well. Think back to exactly what made you select the particular suit or dress you last bought. Was it the superb fit that made you look great (personal enhancement, sex appeal or the appearance of status or power)? Was it the fine quality, tailoring or durable fabric that would make it last for years (value)? Would that garment give you the image of being wealthier (status or power)? Was it fashionable ('fitting in' with the crowd)? Did you buy it simply to keep yourself warm and dry (self-preservation)? You bought that suit or dress because one of those benefits, as noted in the brackets above, appealed to your own need enough to motivate you to buy. You could see, feel or imagine how you would get value from owning that particular garment.

That's what your prospective customers want to know most — how they will get value out of your product or service. The one question that customers always ask themselves is, 'What's in it for me?' Benefits are the 'sparkle' that arouse customers' interest, engage their emotions, and get them to buy from you. You need to present those benefits in all your selling efforts, and back them up with selling points that support the benefits.

What is a selling point?

A selling point is any product or service feature that enables you to deliver the promised benefit or that contributes to that benefit. Selling points are reasons why that result — the benefit — can be produced. The product or service you offer delivers the benefits because of the selling points. Selling points are inherent in the product or service whether or not the customer buys. It is only *after* the sale is made that the customer gets the benefits.

A brief example will show how benefits and selling points work together in the process of a sale. An advertisement for one of the new personal stereo units sets out the benefits and selling points listed below. Notice how each benefit offered is supported by at least one selling point that explains how or why that benefit will be delivered:

Benefit	Selling points
Portability You can enjoy it wherever you go	— self-contained batteries — lightweight — compact — rugged construction
Private You don't have to disturb other people	— sensitive volume control — well insulated headphones

A chart in which you can write down the benefits and selling points of your product or service is included later in this chapter. In doing your own analysis, remember that the more specific you can make your selling points, the more convincing they will be.

Benefits and selling points can be outlined in two ways. You can relate them to the product or service itself, or to the advantages a customer would gain by doing business with *you* rather than with a competitor. Samples of different benefits and selling points that could apply to your business are included in the success worksheet. Before you can choose the benefits that would work best in selling for you, you need to know more about what motivates customers to buy.

Which of these 10 buying motives could you sell to?

Almost all of the complex reasons that people give for buying products or services stem from one or more of the following 10 'emotional' buying motives in some form. Even in the buying of industrial products, some element of these motivators usually creeps in. Most selling appeals that succeed speak to one or more of these 10 major areas of self-interest:

1. Self-preservation
This is the most basic need motivator. On the personal level, self-preservation involves buying such necessities as food, clothing, shelter, and products relating to safety or health.

On the business level, self-preservation often motivates people to buy products or services that will help them keep their jobs, either through making the work easier to do or making them appear more effective and successful to their bosses or colleagues.

Does your product or service help customers fill this basic need in some way?

2. Sex
Sex, or the enhancement of one's attractiveness or sex appeal, can be a powerful motivator. People buy many things in order to feel more beautiful or handsome, more lovable or to evoke warmth or admiration in others.

Does your product offer customers the opportunity to obtain this kind of benefit?

3. Emulation (wanting to be like something or someone)
Many people would love to be like the rich and famous; many have some hidden ideal, such as status or prestige, that they wish to live up to. These people look for products and services that will fulfil those ideals and make them more like the person or ideal they yearn for.

16

Emulation is the factor that accounts for the success of testimonial ads from rich people, film stars and rock stars. The customer is supposed to think, 'If Soandso uses Elite soap, maybe I should buy it and use it so I'll be more like her.'

It may sound ridiculous when described this way, but in reality emulation can be a dynamic motivator. It can work in business situations the same way as in personal lives. Many manufacturers and consultants put lists of their biggest or most powerful clients into their advertising or sales promotion material so that buyers in smaller companies will think, 'If the big companies have used this, maybe it will help *me* grow bigger. If it's good enough for them, it's good enough for me.'

Do you have, or could you get, influential local customers to endorse your product or service?

4. Following the crowd or being 'in style'

Many customers are influenced to buy by wanting to fit in, to be fashionable, or to be like other people in their social or economic groups (or those they wish to join). It is a different type of motivation from emulation, in that following the crowd involves fitting in with a group, rather than imitating someone or something that is exceptional or above the norm.

Though people like to be treated as individuals in a selling situation, you will often find a deep-seated desire to conform, to 'have what the other person has', and to be part of a crowd.

5. Having the best

This motivator involves snob appeal in its many refined and unrefined forms. It can be a powerful selling tool if used well. Many people identify themselves with their possessions, their activities, and their surroundings. They feel that if they have or do the best things that money can buy, they *are* the best.

To use this motivator effectively, you must have a product or service that is fairly exclusive, probably expensive, and definitely top quality. Fine jewellers and top fashion stores catering to the 'carriage trade' are the most obvious examples of businesses using this type of selling appeal. Yet we have seen this quality-based approach used equally well in selling heavy industrial products, home goods, building supplies, drinks, cosmetics, power tools, financial services, and sales training programmes, among others.

Does your product or service offer customers the benefit of having (or dealing with) the best?

6. Being liked or accepted

Most customers want to be liked, or at least accepted, by the people they live and work with. People also buy products or services that will help them avoid the converse of being accepted — that is, being embarrassed, unpleasing or unlikable. Look closely at advertising for toothpaste, mouthwash, deodorants, and courses that promise customers improved conversational skills.

Believe it or not, this benefit can be subtly used in selling some business-oriented products as well. Bosses like to be liked, too. Manufacturers of copying machines and word processors have often appealed to the implied logic that 'if you make your secretary's work easier by buying our product, you will be a considerate, more popular boss'. That's the appeal that often lies below the stated benefits of faster and better work flow.

Is there anything in your product or service that could make your customers feel more likable, or prevent them from feeling unacceptable? Could a form of this appeal be used in your sales?

7. Gaining knowledge and skills

There is a substantial and growing market of people who want to get ahead, improve themselves, add to the quality of their lives, learn more, and be a better/richer/more expert/more skilled/more intelligent person. Indeed, the increase in demand for business and personal self-improvement products has been an outstanding sales phenomenon over the past 10 years. Look at the success of self-improvement books, correspondence courses, management workshops, seminars, and educational cassettes and videotapes for home or office use. People want to learn about everything, from gardening and management techniques to languages and personal financial planning. Customers are willing to invest significant sums in the products or services that will help them master new skills.

Does your product or service help someone to do something better, either personally or professionally? If so, stress all the benefits you can that will appeal to this strong buying motive.

8. Fulfilling a dream

Every customer has a little fantasy picture book inside his or her mind filled with daydreams and wishes. Customers have pictures of how they would like to dress, what they would like to own, how they would like to live, things they want to do, and much more. They have daydreams about what would make

18

them feel valued, rich or pampered. Many of the finer beauty salons, clothing manufacturers, art or antique dealers, and sellers of vintage wines, *objets d'art*, and vintage or luxury cars are well aware of this customer buying motive, and sell to customer fantasy pictures.

Not all fantasies are exotic or involve rare items. Many customer daydreams are far more everyday — things like getting the loft converted or taking a holiday in the sun next winter.

Can you find out what customer daydreams your product or service might cater to, and tie your benefits into this rich and hidden mental world? It could prove pure gold in sales for you.

9. *Getting value for money*

Almost everyone, even the incredibly rich, likes to feel that he or she has made a good deal. Customers like to feel that what they have bought has real value, preferably more than their money's worth. Often, people will even buy things they don't really need, but want to have, because of the value they perceive in buying that product or service. Value can be related to price, to rarity, to long-term savings, to quality, to an improvement in the customer's life-style or prestige. The customer's wish to get value is part of almost every purchase other than 'fun' or impulse buys or the most basic of food and household staples.

If you want to sell with integrity, and build repeat business, you must make sure that your product or service delivers the value your customer expects and has paid for. Otherwise, customers will feel cheated. Part of the process of selling is finding out what the customer expects from your product or service. Methods for getting this information are covered in the chapter on selling techniques.

Are you certain that your product or service will honestly fill your customers' needs and expectations? You will not get re-orders from people who have been disappointed.

10. *Showing them and other revenge motives*

These motivators are not as positive as the others, but they can be even more powerful. Often people who grew up feeling belittled, plain, poor, insecure, unloved, or unworthy buy products or services strictly to show everyone that they really are worthwhile and successful people. This can often be the unconscious motive behind wanting the best.

Are you sensitive to these motives, even though your customers do not say anything about them?

Who will need and buy what you sell?

The benefits you offer, and the buying motives to which those benefits could appeal, will give you the first indicators of who your customers would be. Common sense backed up by simple consumer research will guide you in fitting your product or service more accurately into the customer needs in your own local market.

Before you can complete the success analysis worksheets at the end of this chapter, you need to look closely at two other factors that will affect your sales success: how often you can resell your product or service and who else is competing with you for the customer's money (both directly and indirectly).

Being aware of your selling cycle and competitive activity will help you plan your sales efforts so they reach the right customers at the right time with the benefits that will most make them wish to buy from *you*.

The higher your price, or the less essential your offering, the more important these timing and competitive factors become. Household staples and packaged goods, such as food, personal care products, and cosmetics, can be sold any time and have a short life-cycle. Some heavy industrial goods or specialised consultancy services, on the other hand, may be a once-in-a-lifetime purchase for a business.

How you can find out when people will buy from you

If you are already in business, your own satisfied customers can be your best source of information on timing. They can also tell you which of their friends or colleagues would be interested in your product or service, and when.

If you're new to the market, ask people. Every product or service has a specific, and usually well-defined, life-cycle or use-cycle. This cycle varies according to:

(a) How simple or complex the product or service is
(b) How long that product or service will continue to be of real value to the customer, or how long it will work
(c) Whether the technology, styling, design or service will become obsolescent, outdated, or replaceable by a better product or service

(d) The traditional customer buying patterns in relation to your product or service (Do customers buy once a week, once a month, once a year?)

The longer the lifespan of your product, the more you have to go after new prospects and customer groups to increase your sales. Also remember that the higher your price, the longer it is likely to take most people to decide to buy. People take longer to replace higher-priced products and services, particularly if the purchase involves either outside financing (a bank loan etc) or extensive internal re-financing (such as transferring funds between various divisions within a business to pay for new equipment or services).

Although customers of your own and competitive products are the best source for information on timing, you can also check the following sources:

Manufacturers of products you sell (or want to sell) and their competitors. Most manufacturers know from experience and research how long their products will last, how often they can be resold, and who the primary customer groups are. Look on their packages or in their advertising for where to call. Ask for a salesperson or the sales manager. If you're already established in business, ask the sales reps who regularly call on you.

Trade associations, clubs or professional groups in your industry. Almost every type of business or industry in the United Kingdom has some kind of group representing its interests. Many of these groups publish reference information that could help you manage your business or sell more effectively. The information will normally be available from the association's headquarters. You can get their address or telephone number from trade directories that are kept in the reference section of your local library.

Your local library. Check in the business and reference sections for information. They may have specific facts and research on your type of business, or they could order the information you want from a larger branch.

How businesses can use selling cycles

A few examples will show you how important knowledge of selling cycles can be to your selling efforts.

1. A retail case history

Alan runs a home improvement centre that sells everything from light bulbs and nuts and bolts to luxury kitchen cabinets and bathroom fixtures. He has watched customer buying patterns in the centre, and has found that customers will come in to restock smaller items such as light bulbs, smaller tools, household supplies and inexpensive do-it-yourself items on average every three months.

Alan 'sells into' that pattern by having a quarterly bits and pieces promotion. He sends out direct mail shots and puts up prominent displays around the centre featuring all his impulse lines — and tying them into the larger related products he sells. He features his drill bits on sale next to his higher-priced power and hand drills, which often gives the staff an opportunity to sell the customer a better (and higher priced) drill than he or she currently owns.

Kitchen cabinets, major appliances, and bathroom fixtures have a life-cycle of eight years and more, so he relies on customer referrals and selected direct mail advertising to get new business and new customer names.

Between those two extremes are items like medium-sized power tools, paints, varnishes and stains, more expensive hand tools, and decorative hardware. Though the actual life-cycle for these types of product is around three years, the customer buying patterns tend to run shorter, closer to one or two years, as they buy supplies for new building projects. Alan has found that if he advertises this type of product during the spring and summer repair/redecoration peak seasons, he can sell into customer needs for do-it-yourself projects around the home.

He also backs up his advertising with extensive in-store promotions and direct mail catalogues, which feature the shorter life-cycle products as loss leaders, to bring people into the centre.

If you are a retailer, your sales records, supplier orders, and delivery notes will tell you the life-cycles of your products and lines. You can tell from your turnover how often customers buy each item from you and what the peak seasons are for each category of product you sell. Analyse that information, and use it to plan your advertising and promotional efforts accordingly.

2. A consultancy service case history

Jane is a direct mail copywriter who also does marketing consultancy for a number of small businesses involved in mail-order selling. Most of her new business customers come to her through personal referrals from her own clients.

In Jane's business, the two peak seasons are from early February to late April (when clients are preparing their spring mailings) and from late August to late November (when clients are preparing Christmas mailings). For the direct mail part of her business, Jane's dead seasons are December and January, then May to August.

Jane has learned from experience to plan her time accordingly. She makes her new business sales presentations during the May to August period, and takes her holidays in December or January. To keep her cash flow solid during slack seasons, she has taken three marketing consultancy clients on a monthly fee basis throughout the year to serve as her income base. During May and June, she also advertises a job application writing service for graduating students at the local college of higher education to help them get summer or full-time jobs.

Jane has planned her entire work schedule and cash flow around the known buying patterns of her customer groups. You can do the same analysis by looking at your own books, invoices, and cash flow variations. Not all consultancy services have seasons as pronounced and variable as Jane's.

You have probably also encountered situations where your client no longer needs your services, and you must replace the business. Look for patterns in the work flow and need cycles in all your accounts. Then you can plan for new business presentations well in advance, according to how long it takes new customers to sign up for your consultancy services.

3. A heavy equipment and industrial commercial sales case history

Sara's company sells commercial air purifiers, humidifiers and deodorisers to industrial firms, restaurants, some retail outlets (eg, fish markets, grocery shops, etc) and some hotels. Since the life-cycle of her products is usually 10 years or longer, she puts most of her effort into generating leads for new business through advertising and referrals.

She uses a combination of enquiry generating ads in the trade publications serving her customer markets and a referral campaign working with her current customers. The advertising features an information booklet showing how her products will benefit potential customers, plus a small gift for the customer's office or desk upon reply.

When Sara receives the leads, she immediately gives them to the sales staff, who are organised by territories. The salesperson then *personally* delivers the gift plus the booklet. If possible, the salesperson gets the prospect to answer a few short questions, which indicate how ready the prospect is to buy. If the prospect is too busy at that moment, the salesperson asks for a time when the prospect could be reached, and phones back then.

In cases where the prospect is too far away for personal delivery, Sara sends the booklet and gift by special delivery right away, then has the salesperson do a telephone follow-up within one working week.

Sara also keeps track of exactly when customers have bought from her, so she knows when they will be likely to need service calls or replacement parts, as well as when they'll be ready to buy again as newer models become available.

Since her units range in price from £2500 up to £75,000, Sara rightly feels that the extra sales costs involved in such extensive personal contact by salespeople pays off.

For her personal referrals from present customers, Sara uses the same technique with one addition. She also sends the *current* customer a small gift for each referral, whether or not the prospect ends up buying.

Sara calculates that sooner or later each of her customers will give her up to five good prospect referrals over the course of 10 years. For Sara, that represents a *minimum* sales level of £12,500, so she feels that the referral gifts, which cost under £5 each, are a worthwhile investment.

She has found that her gifts, which are usually funny or whimsical but practical too, tend to keep customers involved with her company and that none of her customers submit referral names to her unless there's at least *some* possibility of a sale in the long term.

The gifts have ranged from a set of beer glasses or whisky tumblers with funny sayings on them and humorous award wall plaques, desk sets or paperweights, to special golf tees.

Sara keeps a customer profile sheet on each customer for salespeople to fill in over a period of time. This sheet outlines, as fully as possible, the customer's hobbies, sports, interests, children — anything that will help Sara pick appropriate gifts and remember customer special events, such as birthdays. This may seem like a lot of extra work, but for £2500 and more a sale, wouldn't *you* find it worthwhile?

You, too, can use Sara's techniques to get names and need levels. Your customers or friends can give you the names, addresses or even the phone numbers of their friends and colleagues who would benefit from buying your product or service.

Use competitive analysis to uncover more benefits

Both your timing and the way you present your benefits to customers will depend partly on the competition you face. You need to know who else in your area is selling products or services similar to yours. Check their prices, what they say in their advertising about their offerings (the benefits and selling points *they* use to sell), and how they advertise. Facts you need to find out include:

(a) How many competitors are there?
(b) Are they new or well-established?
(c) Are they larger or smaller than your business?
(d) Are they cutting into any product or service sales areas where you could be selling?
(e) Are their prices higher or lower than yours?
(f) How is your product or service similar to theirs? More important, how is it different, better, more valuable?
(g) Which media (eg, newspapers, TV, radio, leaflets, direct mail, etc) are they using? When and how often?
(h) What customer groups are their ads designed to reach? Are you trying to sell to the same customer groups? Are there other customer groups you could be selling to?
(i) To which buying motives are your competitors appealing?
(j) How many salespeople does each competitor have? How do they sell (eg, from a retail outlet, door-to-door or business-to-business, by telephone, by post)?

In your success analysis worksheets, you will find a section on competitive activity. Get the facts to fill in the section as completely as possible. You will then have a clearer picture of where you stand in comparison with competitors and where you can successfully sell against them. The more competitors you have, the more thought and effort you will have to put into making your shop, product or service stand out from the rest. You need to make your customer groups aware of you in such a way that they will think of you or your business *first* when they are ready to buy, not your competitors.

Even if you are the only business in your area offering what you sell, you will want to keep current customers aware of you and let prospective new customers know who you are and what you sell.

Customer awareness is the first step in building sales. If customers don't know about you, they won't buy from you (unless you're in a shop where people come in off the street to buy — and even then you need a base of steady customers who buy from you regularly). If you are competing with a number of other businesses, you need to find the benefits and selling points that make your business better, memorable or different from the others, then let customers know about them. Advertising people call this technique *positioning*.

Positioning makes you number one

Positioning, put simply, is the art of making your business number one in the minds of your customers. It is getting your business into an important, memorable spot in the customer's mind based on the benefits — the sparkle — you offer. It is called positioning because that is what you do. You analyse the competition. You find a unique position or need in the market place that no other business is filling. Then you promote that position to customers so that they will see *what you will do for them that no one else is doing*.

Your competitive analysis should show you whether you are offering a better product or service, better quality, lower prices, more status, faster delivery, more convenience, or more experience than your competitors. Once you've found your unique and *saleable* benefits, use the selling tools in Chapter 2 to let people know about them. Customers should be convinced even before they step into your business that you will have what they want and that what you offer *is* what they want. Whether you are selling cosmetics, consultancy services, complex industrial equipment, hardware, hats or fish and chips, show customers why they would be better off buying from *you*. Your positioning serves as the context — the framework — into which all your advertising and direct selling efforts should fit. It is the one basic idea about your business that identifies you to your customers and prospects and makes them think of you.

The three business owners mentioned earlier in the chapter all use positioning to build customer awareness and sales. Alan, the home improvement centre owner, noticed that more young families were starting to move into his area. He decided to position his centre as the 'family place' to buy home improvement products and direct his advertising at young families. He encourages parents to bring their children, and has set up a workbench and supervised play area for youngsters. Alan runs periodic contests and promotions for children of customers, as well as their parents. The main benefits his advertising copy always stresses are family savings, better living for the family, family activities involving his products, and the warm welcome the whole family will get in Alan's shop.

Alan chose his position very carefully, based on what he saw his competitors doing and what he felt his customers needed. As he explains, 'Most retailers don't like children in their stores. They run around, get noisy, break things. But those things only happen if the youngster is ignored or bored. I realised that if parents could bring their children in and know that they were being kept busy, the parents would shop longer and buy more. Also, I know that when both parents are in the shop, one often remembers household needs and items that the other forgot. Mum picks up those kitchen gadgets she wants, while dad looks at power tools or paint or supplies to fix the plumbing that mum reminded him about. They both find what they need, and my sales go up. Meanwhile, the youngsters have been happily banging away with small hammers and surplus wood pieces, not bothering anyone. I also stock family games, some family sports equipment and toys, which are all in the aisles leading to and from the play area. Those bring in plenty of impulse sales.'

Alan has supported his positioning as a family centre with everything from advertising and price benefits to products he stocks and where they are displayed. His centre is known as a fun place to take the children while buying what you need for your home and family life. Alan has documented a 15 per cent increase in units sold and a 24 per cent increase in sales revenues over the first year of his positioning campaign.

You can use positioning as a manufacturer, consultant, or door-to-door salesperson, or when you're selling your own skills or services. Jane, the writer/consultant, based her positioning on being able to deliver copy that would get the job done for clients in less time than competitors. Since her advertising clients were always in a hurry for their work, she stressed the benefits that would fill their needs. She, of course, had the talent to back up her claims of fast, result-getting work.

Sara's funny gifts were all part of building a position based on unique personal service, as well as the quality of her products. She uses them both to get sales leads *and* to build awareness of herself and her products in the minds of customers.

How to use your success analysis worksheets

Now that you know about benefits, selling points, buying motives, timing, competition, and positioning, it's time to start putting them to use in building sales. Use the following worksheet to begin.

The worksheet contains the first steps toward building a realistic sales plan. You can't build a plan until you are clear about what you're really selling.

Go through each page and put in as much information as possible. If you don't know about your competition, ask around and find out until you can fill in the worksheet. If you don't know about the replacement time for your product or service, ask the suppliers of your product or potential clients of your service. The more information you have, the more you will be able to put it to use in your sales.

On the benefit analysis pages, tick every benefit that your product or service offers. There will probably be more than one benefit. Then number them in the order of their importance *to your customers*. What you think is important about your product/service may not be what is important to customers. If you're not sure, find out. It's critical that you know which benefits will work best to motivate customers, so you know how to present your benefits in a way that will sell.

This worksheet will give you the basic data you need to *use* the sales tools and selling techniques outlined later in this book. *Don't skip this section.* You will be using it as a basis on which to build your own selling script in Chapters 2 and 3.

SUCCESS ANALYSIS WORKSHEETS

Name of business:_____ Years established:_____
Product(s) or service(s) sold:_____

_____

How is my product/service used?_____

_____

_____

Where would it be used? (Tick those that apply and fill in 'Other'.):

☐ In the home   ☐ Outdoors   ☐ In a shop
☐ In the office   ☐ Indoors   ☐ On construction sites
☐ In a factory   ☐ In a car or boat,   ☐ In hospitals/clinics/
                           truck or caravan   nursing homes/
                                            surgeries

Other:_____

_____

_____

Which customer groups would use or need my product/service?

☐ Business owners   ☐ Skilled tradespeople   ☐ Children
☐ Young families   ☐ Office workers   ☐ Pensioners
☐ Single women   ☐ Managers/supervisors   ☐ Couples
☐ Single men   ☐ Professionals such as   ☐ Teenagers
                             doctors, dentists,
                             solicitors

Other:_____

_____

_____

(If you have more than one prospective customer group, use a separate sheet plus the space below to describe each group in one sentence. An example might be: 'Women aged 18 and over who want to look attractive and prefer natural cosmetics' if you're selling organic cosmetics.)

Benefits/Buying motives

(Notice here how benefits and buying motives tie in together. That's because benefits are the real reasons why customers buy a product or service. Selling points or features are more often brought in after the customer has been emotionally sold by the benefits, as tools to justify the purchase to the customer's mind.)

Here are the benefits my product or service offers:

My product or service will (tick any benefits which apply):

☐ Fill a self-preservation need for the customer.

☐ Make the customer feel more beautiful or handsome, more attractive or sexier.

☐ Make dirty jobs easier for the customer.

☐ Make the customer's home more beautiful or valuable or comfortable.

☐ Give the customer status with friends and neighbours by owning it.

☐ Make the customer feel fashionable, trendy, with it.

☐ Make the customer feel more powerful, affluent or sophisticated.

☐ Make the customer feel more likable or acceptable.

☐ Fulfil a customer's ideals or dreams.

☐ Make the customer feel pampered or cared about.

☐ Help the customer have more fun in life or enjoy life more fully.

☐ Make customers feel valued and worthwhile.

☐ Help the customer keep his or her job.

☐ Help the customer get the work done faster or better.

☐ Make the customer look better to colleagues or bosses.

☐ Make the customer's office more organised, more comfortable, more prestigious-looking or more efficient.

☐ Give the customer more status with colleagues by using it.

☐ Make the customer feel more effective, dynamic, intelligent or skilled in some area.

☐ Make the customer feel like the best in business or personal life.

☐ Improve the quality of a customer's business or personal life.

☐ Assist the customer in developing a new skill or knowledge.

☐ Make the customer feel as if he or she has acquired something rare or of great value.

☐ Empower customers to do, own or be something they have not had or been previously.

Other benefits:_____

_____

Product/Service life cycle and timing analysis

Product Price:_____ Service hourly rate:_____

How often does my product have to be replaced or my service need to be done once more:

☐ Every week   ☐ Every two years
☐ Every few weeks   ☐ From three to five years
☐ Once a month   ☐ From five to 10 years
☐ Once every few months   ☐ Over 10 years
☐ Twice a year   ☐ Never needs replacing once done
☐ Once a year   or bought
☐ Irregularly as customer   ☐ Constantly needs replacing as
   needs arise — no set time   product is used up or service is
                                    performed.

Is there a specific season of the year in which my product or service sells best or is most often used?   ☐ Yes   ☐ No

Is my product or service available year-round? ☐ Yes   ☐ No

Do customers need or want my products or services year-round?   ☐ Yes   ☐ No

Do my competitors offer their products/services more or less frequently than I do?

_____

Is there a specific time of the week or month during which my product or service best fills customer needs?

_____

When is (are) the best time(s) to contact customers about my product or services? Do I contact them at that time?

_____

POSITIONING STATEMENT

Write one sentence (or two) that best describes where and how your product, service (or shop) best fits into the market place:

_____

_____

(Examples: I sell the best organic cosmetics available to women who want natural beauty products. My shop is the family centre for building supplies and hardware.)

Competitive situation analysis

Competitor	Size	Their benefits	My benefits	How I can sell against them

1. Most important: _____

No. of salespeople: _____

Which of my customer groups are they reaching? _____

Where are they advertising? _____

How could I offer more than they do? _____

2. Second most important: _____

No. of salespeople: _____

Which of my customer groups are they reaching? _____

Where are they advertising? _____

How could I offer more than they do? _____

3. Third most important: _____

No. of salespeople: _____

Which of my customer groups are they reaching? _____

Where are they advertising? _____

How could I offer more than they do? _____

Are there other competitors I should watch? _____

What do I know about my competitors concerning:

Their benefits: _____   Their advertising: _____

Their customer groups: _____   Quality of their product(s)/service(s): _____

Their pricing: _____   Positioning: _____

Timing: _____

WHAT COULD I DO TO GET MORE SALES AND COMPETE MORE EFFECTIVELY?
(Fill in this section after you have completed reading this entire book.)

In advertising:

In personal and telephone selling:

In promotion:

In community public relations:

In my product, pricing, services:

In any other ways:

In finding new customers:

Selling points and features analysis:

These are the qualities and features that make it possible for your product or service to deliver the benefits the customer is buying. They represent the logical, rather than the emotional reasons to buy. Tick off all those listed which apply, then add any other specific selling points that could be added to describe your own product, service or store:

My product offers:
- ☐ Quality
- ☐ Durability
- ☐ Elegance
- ☐ Beauty
- ☐ Style
- ☐ Workmanship
- ☐ Colours
- ☐ Size convenience
- ☐ Hand finishing
- ☐ Antique
- ☐ Contemporary
- ☐ Easy to use
- ☐ Easy to install
- ☐ Convenient weight
- ☐ Easy to carry
- ☐ Efficient functioning
- ☐ Special finish
- ☐ Strength
- ☐ Variety of colours
- ☐ Variety of sizes
- ☐ Movable parts
- ☐ Easy to clean
- ☐ Investment value

My service offers:
- ☐ Specialised knowledge
- ☐ Specialised skills
- ☐ Experience in the field
- ☐ Efficient service
- ☐ Fast service
- ☐ Top quality service
- ☐ Availability of service
- ☐ Convenient service hours
- ☐ Flexible service hours
- ☐ Uniqueness of service
- ☐ Luxury of service
- ☐ Cost-efficiency of service
- ☐ Timeliness of service

My shop offers:
- ☐ Wide range of products
- ☐ Depth of stock
- ☐ Top quality products
- ☐ Low prices
- ☐ Convenient shopping hours
- ☐ Convenient location
- ☐ Good customer service
- ☐ Free delivery

The selling points above were listed just to get you started. Now take the space below to make a more specific list for your own product, service or shop:

_____

_____

_____

_____

_____

_____

_____

SUCCESS ANALYSIS SUMMARY SHEET

Portrait of your product, service or shop

This sheet is where you put together what you have discovered so far. Do this exercise to determine which aspects of your product, service or shop are most important in building sales.

Product or service: _____

My most important benefits are: _____

_____

_____

Most important selling points that support those benefits: _____

_____

_____

Timing of my selling cycle: _____

Competitive advantages: _____

_____

_____

Any other factors about my product, service or shop which I know could help me sell: _____

_____

_____

_____

_____

_____

_____

_____

_____

_____

_____

_____

_____

_____

_____

_____

_____

Chapter 2

Enlarging Your Customer Base

Now that you have analysed what your product or service has to offer, you need to find the customers to sell to.

Three sources of increased sales

Whether you are in door-to-door, retail, industrial, product or service selling, your potential for new or increased sales will come from these three customer-related sources.

1. New customers
These are people you don't yet know, though you may know who they are and where to find them. They are prospects who want or need and can afford what you offer, but may not know about you or your business. Building new business generally involves more time, effort, and money per sale than working with established customers who already know you.

2. Getting existing customers to buy more often
Your objectives for increasing sales should include plans for converting your light users or buyers into medium or heavy users. In fast-moving consumer goods (foods and household staples), many manufacturers use coupons, premiums, and special offers to bring in repeat sales faster. Look for ways to get customers buying more frequently in order to get a further benefit. For example, the Dairy Council promoted sales of cream by offering one free pack to consumers who bought two packs of cream during a limited period. Customers come back for that.

3. Getting current customers to buy more per order
Selling related products or services can increase the average value of each sale. For example, car parts retailers group spark plugs, points and a feeler gauge together as a package and sell it as a tune-up kit.

This chapter is about techniques you can use to build up a customer base that will expand your sales from all three sources. You will also calculate your business drawing power and get a checklist of 30 local sources of new customer groups from which your business could get sales.

Four things customers or prospects should always be told

Your job is to show each of your important customer or prospect groups exactly how your product or service will do one or more of the following:

(a) Bring them the end results they are looking for.
(b) Prove well worth the money they are investing in your product or service (either as opposed to not buying at all or to buying from your competitors).
(c) Offer them the quality, value, service or other benefits that customers have a right to expect from your business.
(d) Meet their business or personal needs.

Techniques for selling more to current customers

The key to increasing sales from current customers is to keep in touch. If you are not there, you will not sell to them. Even when a customer or client has stopped buying from you, or has had a bad or unsatisfactory experience with you, keep in touch. You might be able to soften the client's attitude towards your business and keep that client from saying bad things about you to your other prospects. You may be able to correct that negative impression over time and even make another sale to that client — but only if you stay in touch.

If you see news about a customer's business, family, or career (such as an appointment notice in your local paper), use it as an excuse to remind that customer of you. Enclose your business card with a short note saying 'congratulations on your new baby' or 'good luck in your new job' as a reminder of you.

Also keep in contact with prospects who did not buy from you before. You can never be completely sure when they will be ready to buy. Keep any coupons or enquiry forms that did not lead to sales the first time. Go over them twice a year, and follow up by telephone or post.

Whenever you decide to offer new products or services, let all your current customers know about them. Use your telephone or the post. Offer them a special introductory price for a limited period as valued customers.

A new product or service also gives you an ideal opportunity to contact dormant accounts — customers who have not bought from you in a year or more. Remind them pleasantly of your past business with them, and introduce your new product or services to re-interest them in you.

Use your staff wisely to get information from current customers about their needs, likes and dislikes, their families, what is important to them, reasons why they buy, and other factors that could affect your sales. The more you know about your current customers, the more you can build sales and goodwill even when customers are not in your business premises.

You don't always have to celebrate personal customer events to remind customers of you. Use the anniversary of the opening of the customer's account with you, or a local civic event to remind him or her of your business. These gestures may seem like a lot of unnecessary trouble to you, but the returns they can bring in goodwill, customer awareness, and *sales* can prove extremely worthwhile for you.

Let current customers lead you to new ones

Once you have canvassed your current customers and done your best to increase sales to them, look for new customer groups with similar characteristics. Once you have sold to one doctor, you have the tools and techniques you need to sell to other doctors.

You can ask your current customers for names of their friends or colleagues who would be interested in what you sell. The techniques for generating leads and referrals are covered in detail in the next section.

Once you have determined who your best new prospect groups could be, you can use one or more of the following techniques to reach them and generate their interest and sales:

1. Introduce yourself to new people in the district
Look through your newspaper and neighbourhoods for new businesses, families moving into town, families with new babies, newlyweds — any new people who fit your general customer profiles. A quick phone call saying welcome or congratulations will let prospects know you are around. Keep it friendly, brief and relaxed.

2. Hand out leaflets or business cards

Leave leaflets, mailing pieces or your business cards at offices, shopping centres, industrial estates, supermarkets — wherever you go where prospects are likely to be found. Keep a supply with you everywhere you go. You never know when you'll see a prospect. Drop them through the letter boxes of group 1 above.

3. Do a telephone campaign

Have a staff member call businesses or families at random to see if they buy the types of products or services that you sell. Chapter 3 will show you how to rank prospects, make appointments with them, or even generate sales with telephone prospecting techniques.

4. Hold a contest or event to bring new customers to you

Chapters 4 to 6 give you the promotional tools and ideas you can use to get customers into your business. Direct your efforts at the neighbourhoods or business districts most likely to contain prospective customers for your product or service.

5. Offer free booklets, information or gifts

Get people to give you their names by sending in a coupon from your advertising or calling your business to get free items. Follow up each new lead immediately. As well as the free item, send them whatever information or assistance they would need to consider buying from you.

6. Use the next section to generate leads and referrals

The next few pages explain what leads and referrals are, how to get them, and how to sell to them. These prospective customers are an important part of your customer base.

Leads and referrals — your business lifeblood

There are two groups of potential customers who offer you the best possible selling opportunities. These two groups are called leads and referrals.

1. Leads

Leads are prospective customers; they are people you come across in situations that can lead to a sale. A lead does one of the following things:

(a) Walks into your shop or business off the street and enquires about something or looks around.
(b) Answers your advertising or requests more information.
(c) Brings in one of your coupons, gift tokens, or entry forms or a contest.
(d) Phones you or your sales staff to ask about your products or services.
(e) Takes away catalogues, specification sheets or product/service brochures to look at further.

A lead does not necessarily want or need to buy. The fact that customers show interest may or may not mean they're currently in the market. Depending on the life cycle of your product or service, it may take a prospect anywhere from a day to a month to a year to be emotionally and logically *prepared* to buy.

Get names and follow up regularly. When a person calls or walks into your premises, get his or her name if at all possible, and find out where to get in touch with him or her. Try as subtly as possible, *without pushing*, to get information on what each prospect is looking for and how close he or she is to buying (or signing up for your services).

If you can't get information, do your best to get them interested enough to take away some materials that will remind them of your business.

Retailers and manufacturers can use product brochures, specification sheets, booklets, even advertising tear sheets. Service businesses and consultants should have general brochures outlining their credentials, types of services, and customer benefits.

Give out your own business card as often as you can. It is often less threatening to the prospect than larger information pieces. If the prospect is interested, he or she is likely to keep your card for future reference. Your card should have some reference to what you sell or do, either in your shop or business name, your own title, or a note you write on the card.

2. Referrals: making your customers work for you
A referral is the name of a prospective customer given to you by one of your own satisfied customers who knows the prospect. Usually the referred prospect will be in a similar business or personal situation as your own customer or will have similar interests.

Keep in mind that the higher the price and the more the customer is satisfied with his or her purchase, the more likely he or she is to tell friends and colleagues about it. That kind of word of mouth won't help you sell as much as having those friends' and colleagues' names to follow up yourself.

The best time (but not the only time) to get customer referrals is with the purchase (or contract). This might be at the time of sale (or signing). It might also be after a month of product use or service performed, so the client or customer has a better chance to experience the benefits of your product or service.

3. Comparing leads and referrals

Referrals are usually more productive than leads. You are four to six times more likely to close a sale on a good referral than you are to close on a walk-in lead.

Why is this so? Here are five good reasons:

You have an introduction to the prospect. You have your own customer's name to use as a door-opener to get the prospect interested faster. You also have that name to encourage the prospect to find out more about you from his or her colleague.

You know something about the prospect. You have enough information about the prospect from your own customer to find out quickly whether the need and desire for your product or service exists now, or could be built up in a fairly short time.

The word may already have got around. If the purchase made or service performed was major or extraordinary in some way, the customer is already likely to have discussed it with friends who are in the same personal circumstances or line of business as he or she is. In that case, you would be less likely to be calling cold (unknown to the prospect) on your customer's referral names.

Your customer can introduce you. In some businesses, you can get your own customer to work even more actively for you by having him or her call the prospect to introduce you. This technique can be particularly effective to break the ice if you're in industrial or commercial sales or working as a consultant or freelance service person.

You can cross-refer with non-competitors. Another variation of the referral process can be cross-referring good clients with non-competitors. As marketing consultants, we often come across clients who need the services of good artists, production people, or other consultants in accounting or personal services. We introduce the appropriate service people to our clients wherever possible as an extra dimension of our services. Sometimes that encourages the client or the other service person either to find more business for us or to refer their colleagues to us.

We have discovered that the more generous we are in referring clients to others who could benefit them, the more good business we get in return over the long run — even if it is from indirect sources. The word does get around.

4. *How can you find out how good a referral is?*

Ask. It's the only way. Whether or not you can get the information from your own customer, the real source is the prospect. You need to ask as many questions as possible, in a relaxed way. Do your best to ask questions that don't give the prospect a chance to turn off or say no.

Some of the questions you might ask include your own variations of the following. Adapt these to your own product or service.

(a) Are you thinking of immediate needs or more long-range needs?
(b) Do you prefer that model in the white or the blue?
(c) Does your company prefer to use this type of service on a monthly, quarterly or yearly basis?
(d) Do you feel you'd prefer to look at this again in three months or six months?
(e) Are you interested more in economy or in fast service?
(f) Is quality your main concern, or are you interested more in the cost per unit?

There are endless ways to ask questions that involve the customer and get him or her talking to you. Three points to remember when you're talking to a lead or a prospect are:

Relax: Don't rush, act harried, get tense, or ask questions as if your life depended on it. Customers shy away from tense or pushy questions and tend to go elsewhere.

Learn to listen: Once you have a prospect involved and talking, *listen*. The prospect will be telling you about the needs and desires your business can serve, his or her problems and objections to past products and services purchased, and how close you are to a sale.

You have probably seen salespeople literally talk themselves out of a sale by not hearing what the prospect is saying. You may also have seen salespeople harp on about *economy* when the customer wants *value at any price* — and lose a sale. We have watched salespeople talk their way out of opportunities to sell to a prospect who is ready to buy.

Don't interrupt a prospect or change the subject if the prospect brings up something that is uncomfortable or doesn't fit into your usual presentation routine. Answer the questions or objections fully as they occur. Only then can you ask another question that will get the prospect back into your selling track.

Make sure you understand the prospect completely: Again, use questions or confirmations to make absolutely certain that you and the prospect understand each other, and are communicating on the same wavelength.

Phrase it so the prospect can either agree with you or correct your misunderstanding right away. Here are some examples of this type of technique:

(a) Do I understand correctly that you would prefer the model with the x, y and z options?
(b) Let me go over this again, (prospect name). You want the regular bookkeeping functions performed each month, plus a special tax accounting service at the end of your financial year each December. Am I correct?
(c) Do I have it right that you prefer to make your company's investment in this product on a quarterly basis?
(d) Would it be accurate to say that you expect about a 10 per cent increase in your sales if you invest in this equipment?

Make sure that everything is clear between you and the prospect *as you go along*. Otherwise, you'll probably encounter a hidden objection just when you are ready to close the sale. (Handling those objections is covered in more detail in the next chapter on selling techniques.) Save yourself some time by clarifying the prospect's needs at each stage of your discussion.

Once you have concluded a satisfactory transaction, you can ask the prospect, now a customer, for referrals to other people who could buy. Keep in mind that the average person you meet has knowledge of or contact with about 250 people in his or her life, including family and relatives, friends, neighbours, business acquaintances, doctors, school friends, sports team mates, fellow club members, competitors, and people who serve his or her family or business. Treat each new and current customer as a source of referral business, and you will build up your customer base that much faster.

30 Local sources of new customer groups

Once you have increased the sales to your current customers and followed up their referrals and your other leads, you will want to look for new business as part of your customer base. Groups of people, eg, clubs, associations etc, are one important source of business that many small business owners overlook. If you have sold your product or service to one member of a club or group, you can probably sell to others.

This section contains a list of 30 sources for new prospects. You may have overlooked them in your search for new sales. As you go through the list, compare the members you know in any of the groups or sources with your own customer profiles. Do they fit? Could they fit? Could their needs be the same as those of your most important prospect/customer groups? Could they relate enough to the benefits and features you outlined for your product or service to buy what you sell?

Keep those possibilities in mind as you read this section, then check off the appropriate groups in the worksheet at the end of this chapter.

Look through and see if there *are* groups who would buy from you that you aren't reaching now. Your approach to new customers and the benefits you offer them should be tailored to your own selling situation and their needs or desires for your products or services.

1. Types of clubs or groups from which to get member names

Each type of group listed here has a membership list full of potential new customer names. If you already belong to a club or group, you'll have a much easier way to reach other members and build rapport with them, based on your common interests. If not, you may still be able to obtain their membership lists for your mailings, providing your offer would be of real value to club members.

1. Church groups, missionary societies, church memberships
2. Social clubs and special interest groups
3. Civic groups
4. Local trade associations or professional clubs
5. Service clubs, such as Rotary, Round Table etc
6. Local and national business groups, such as the Chamber of Commerce, small business clubs
7. Local trade union branches and political parties

8. Gardening clubs, horticultural societies and Young Farmers' groups
9. Savings clubs
10. YMCAs, YWCAs, YHAs
11. Ex-service or veterans' clubs, especially your local branch of the British Legion
12. Ladies' or gentlemen's clubs, executive clubs
13. Sports, health or fitness clubs
14. Charter travel clubs
15. Women's Institutes, Townswomen's Guilds, Mothers' Union, Cooperative Women's Guild, etc.

2. Lists and/or directories you could rent or obtain

16. List brokers

In larger towns or cities, you may find it easier to deal with a professional list broker. Generally listed under Advertising — Direct Mail in your Yellow Pages, these professionals make it their entire business to build, maintain and keep accurate lists of specific customer groups for advertisers. They will sell or rent a list of names of current customers for your products, if such a list has been compiled. If you tell them exactly what you want, they can often compile a list specifically for you, although this is generally much more expensive.

A list broker can save you a lot of headaches, at anything from £35 to £100 per 1000 names. Large brokers usually require a minimum commitment of 5000 names, unless a specific list is shorter. Direct mailing houses will often mail to specific target groups. Ensure that your own (return) address is printed on the envelope, as the Post Office is not obliged to open up and return undelivered second class mail. This keeps the list updated, and the mailing house should credit you with any returns. Keep track of the sales generated.

17. Electoral register
18. Chamber of Commerce directories
19. Book clubs, football pools promoters, motoring organisations and mail order companies may allow non-competing organisations access to their membership lists.
20. Credit card holder lists. Local credit account companies like departmental stores are more likely than national companies to allow you to enclose your mailing shot with their monthly statements or other customer mailings.
21. Professional societies' reference books and directories

22. Registration or delegate lists from conferences or exhibitions
23. Business or industrial directories for your locality.

3. New customer lists you can probably make up yourself

24. Your friends and colleagues

Your tennis or football club, bridge club, golf, playing acquaintances, fellow club members and social acquaintances could all be customers if your business serves their needs.

25. People who serve you

This includes professionals such as your doctor, solicitor, accountant, bookkeeper, and dentist. Depending on the nature of your business, this list can include anyone from the local car mechanic and supermarket staff, to the car dealer or furniture salespeople you rely on, to the estate agent who helped you find or sell your home. Don't forget your insurance broker, bank staff, and other personal suppliers who have your business.

26. Friends and contacts of your employees and/or shareholders
27. Supplier recommendations

Sometimes your suppliers can suggest other business people or personal friends that your business could be serving.

28. People who have answered your ads or promotions (or who have phoned you) but haven't bought from you before

Look up your past enquiries or responses and contact them again. If you don't have records of enquiries, start keeping them now.

29. Revive your own past accounts

Look through past delivery notes, invoices, salespeople's call reports and credit records to find old customers or clients who haven't bought from you in some time.

30. List exchanges with non-competitive but comparable businesses

Keeping your lists up to date

Unless your list is kept current, it will be of little value to you. Customers who aren't there don't buy. To keep your list up to date, send out periodic mailings to the entire list. Your returns will tell you which customers have moved, died, or just don't want direct mail. Then have someone go through the master list and take out all of those returns.

In a small or rural community, you can probably get away with three- or six-month periods between updating. In a large city, however, your list should probably be updated at least monthly.

Of course, you'll probably get a few returns each time you send out your mail shots or advertising. If you keep your records up to date each time you mail, you'll have much less trouble keeping your list active.

One last point: unless you use your list *regularly* to generate sales, you will be wasting your time. But you will see how worthwhile the time you've spent is when you consider that a carefully planned, well-aimed direct mail or advertising campaign can:

(a) Act as your sales representative in print
(b) Bring people into your shops or premises to buy
(c) Generate goodwill
(d) Keep you in your customers' minds, and
(e) Help you sell.

Every name on a *good* mailing list can mean sales for you.

WORKSHEET FOR BUILDING A CUSTOMER BASE FOR INCREASED SALES

1. Which of the three sources of increased sales is most likely for my business right now?

   By how much?

   ☐ Finding and selling to new customer groups. _____
   ☐ Selling to current customers *more often*. _____
   ☐ Selling *more per order* to current customers. _____

2. What specifically can I do to accomplish the above objective?

   _____

3. Rank the 30 sources of new prospect groups in order of their possible importance to your business, and say why. Use 0 to denote groups of no importance, 10: most important, etc.

Group	*Rank*	*Why this group is important*
1. Church groups	_____	_____
2. Social clubs	_____	_____
3. Civic groups	_____	_____
4. Trade associations	_____	_____
5. Service clubs	_____	_____
6. Business groups	_____	_____
7. Trade unions/ political parties	_____	_____
8. Gardening clubs	_____	_____
9. Savings clubs	_____	_____
10. YMCA/YWCA/ YHA	_____	_____
11. Ex-service/ veterans groups	_____	_____
12. Private clubs	_____	_____
13. Sports clubs	_____	_____
14. Charter travel clubs	_____	_____
15. Women's Institutes	_____	_____
16. List brokers	_____	_____
17. Electoral register	_____	_____
18. Chambers of Commerce	_____	_____
19. Membership lists	_____	_____
20. Credit card lists	_____	_____
21. Professional societies	_____	_____

WORKSHEET FOR BUILDING A CUSTOMER BASE FOR INCREASED SALES

Group	Rank	Why this group is important
22. Conference delegates	_____	_____
23. Business directories	_____	_____
24. Friends/colleagues	_____	_____
25. Service people	_____	_____
26. Employee contacts	_____	_____
27. Supplier contacts	_____	_____
28. Leads from ads	_____	_____
29. Past accounts	_____	_____
30. List exchanges	_____	_____

4. Here is a contact list of the people I already know in the 10 groups I have ranked as most important to my business. These are people I can contact to get sales, leads and referrals:

Group	Person's name	Phone number	When I'll phone
_____	_____	_____	_____
_____	_____	_____	_____
_____	_____	_____	_____
_____	_____	_____	_____
_____	_____	_____	_____

— — — — —

5. Here is a list of other people I know who could assist me in finding new prospects or getting new sales:

_____

_____

_____

_____

_____

— — — — —

Chapter 3

Techniques for Face-to-Face and Telephone Selling

The sale itself is the heart of the matter. You can be completely knowledgeable about your product/service, your customer groups, your marketing area, and how they all fit together, but if you can't make the sale, your efforts have been wasted.

This chapter is about closing the sale, whether you are with the customer in person or on the telephone. You will find out why prospects don't buy, how to tell when a prospect *is* ready to buy, how to handle objections, and a few more ways to increase sales. The second part of this chapter focuses on using the telephone as a powerful tool in generating both referrals and actual sales.

The techniques in this chapter can be used by any business person to sell any product or service. Do not skip any of this chapter. Even if you don't think a specific case history or idea applies to you, the underlying principle does. You can always adapt the principle to your own specific situation. These are proven techniques that have worked for thousands of business owners and salespeople. Use as many of them as you possibly can to get the orders and close your sales.

10 Most common reasons why a prospect does not buy

Before analysing the six main steps involved in a sale, here are the most common problems that can prevent you from making a sale:

1. The prospect does not know what he or she needs or wants.
2. The prospect does not know enough about your product or service to make an informed decision to purchase, and so decides not to buy.
3. The prospect doesn't understand or has misinformation about your product or service, which stands in the way of the sale. Wrong information can be a real sale-killer.

4. The prospect is concerned about price, value or payment terms, rather than about the product or service itself. These concerns may or may not be expressed as objections.
5. The prospect already has a satisfactory product/service, or has something in mind, that is similar to your offering but not the same.
6. The prospect has a brand name, a competitor, or a type of product or service in mind that you do not offer.
7. The prospect receives a bad impression of you, your staff, your offering or even your premises, and decides not to buy.
8. Your products or services do not appeal to the prospect. The prospect does not find either what he or she wants or needs or an acceptable substitute.
9. Friends of the prospect have expressed dissatisfaction with your business. Such a 'hidden objection' in the prospect's mind can be difficult to bring out and deal with.
10. The prospect has a valid reason not to buy. You will find that some prospects will shop even when they could not possibly buy. A good salesperson can soon distinguish the difference between an objection or concern that *can* be overcome and a true block to the sale. You and your sales staff must learn to handle a blocked sale gracefully, so that the prospect will be encouraged to return when the block is gone.

10 Ways to tell if a prospect is ready to buy

How can you tell if a prospect will buy? Most customers will give you some indication when they have decided to make a purchase. Train your staff and yourself to be alert to these 10 common indicators that a prospect is serious:

1. The prospect starts asking questions about the product or service. The prospect is interested enough to want to know more. Specific questions about your benefits or selling features, quality, experience, alternative products or services, or prices and payment terms are usually preludes to a buying decision.
2. The prospect expresses a specific desire for a product or service. If prospective customers can be gently induced to tell you what they want, and you do that service or carry that product, you are half-way to the sale. Your selling

task then becomes showing the prospect why or how *your* product or service fills those expressed needs.

3. The prospect raises objections about price, service etc but does not end the conversation. Objections are often a form of interest in your offering. An objection may be another way of getting more information about your product or service, or it may reflect a true barrier to the sale. Find out which. Welcome objections, because if you cannot learn exactly what is stopping your prospect from buying, you probably won't make the sale.

4. The prospect mentions your advertising, or asks for a specific product or service that has been featured in your ads. This often means that the prospect has been motivated enough by the benefits in your advertising to act. Your selling task is to reinforce the benefits your prospect came in to buy, answer any further questions, and pre-qualify further to see that the sale is appropriate.

5. The prospect says he or she has bought before. If prospects tell you that they have previously bought something like what you offer, that may mean that they are ready to buy again. Even if they have had a bad experience, it is an opportunity for you. Once you find out what happened last time, you can show how your product or service will prevent the same thing from happening again.

6. The prospect makes first contact. If the prospect answers an ad, brings in a coupon, telephones you after a radio or TV spot, or writes to you for more information, he or she is usually ready to buy. It may turn out that your product or service is *not* what the prospect really wanted. If not, do whatever you can to satisfy the prospect, even if it means referring him or her to another company. That prospect will then remember you and your honesty when he or she is in the market for a product or service you *do* offer. *Never* lie to a prospect, even if you lose a sale.

7. The prospect is just shopping around. Prospects who are shopping are usually ready to buy. They have not yet found the right combination of price, benefits, and value that sparks their desire to buy. That desire will seldom be based strictly on logic. Usually emotional factors related to the benefits will influence the buying decision. Your selling task here is to get prospects talking about what they really want, so you can build up their desire to own the benefits you offer. Your questions will also reveal how

close each prospect actually is to buying.

8. Prospects are currently using someone else's product or service in your category. They may even be satisfied. But if they are willing to talk to you, they will eventually be in the market again. Never make the mistake of knocking or criticising the competition. It insults prospects, as you are suggesting they made a bad or wrong decision, and you will probably lose the sale. Instead, emphasise ways in which *your* product or service can serve prospects better without making direct comparisons. You can do this through stressing benefits, and asking questions.

9. The prospect brings in the *real* buyer/buying influence. Whether you are selling to a husband who needs his wife's agreement to make a major household purchase, or a marketing manager who must get board approval before granting you a consultancy contract, you don't always contact the real buying influence the first time. When you find yourself in a selling situation where the prospect does not have the ultimate buying authority, find out who does. Your aim is to get the prospect working for you to involve and help sell to that buying influence.

   Give your non-buying prospect all the information and answers on your benefits and selling points you can, preferably in written form. Encourage the prospect to get the real buying influence to speak to you personally as well. *Never* look at these types of prospects as a waste of time. If you treat them well, they will often do most of your preliminary sales work for you. If you can get them to bring in the actual buying influence, you will usually have a sale.

10. The prospect begins agreeing with you. When the prospect agrees with benefit statements you make or with questions you ask, it indicates an open mind. That is the first major step towards a sale. You can build agreement by asking such safe questions as, 'You are interested in value that will appreciate over the years, aren't you?' (Who would answer no to that?)

    Practise a series of safe agreement questions relevant to your product or service. If you alternate that type of question with other questions designed to uncover the prospect's own wants and needs, you can build a body of agreement that could lead you to a mutually satisfying sale.

The six steps to building a sale

As soon as a person walks into your premises or contacts you, you have a prospective customer. To convert that prospect into a customer, you need to go through six main steps. How those steps look, or what exact words you use to accomplish them, will vary according to your specific selling situation. They do not always happen one at a time or in the exact order in which they are set out here. This analysis is organised for the sake of clarity. In real-life selling situations, all six steps are interrelated throughout the process. They are:

1. Get as much information as possible about the prospect's wants or needs — what the prospect is looking for.
2. Relate your product or service specifically to those prospect needs.
3. Show *how* your offering will fill those needs as clearly as possible and why the prospect will get the value expected.
4. Build up a body of agreement with the prospect.
5. Handle the prospect's questions, objections, and considerations to the prospect's satisfaction. This process may include uncovering hidden or unvoiced objections by asking questions.
6. *Ask for the order* and close the sale. You would be astonished how many otherwise good salespeople fail to make this vital step.

When a prospect first walks in or contacts you, your primary aim should be to get as much information as you can without pressuring the prospect. Never ask a question such as 'May I help you?' That is inviting the prospect to say no. Instead, try a question that gives the prospect a choice. In a retail situation, this could be, 'Is there something specific I can show you, or would you rather look around for a while first?' In a service situation, you might ask, 'Is there a specific service that interests you most, or would you rather know more about our company first?' A manufacturer might ask the prospect, 'Do you have a particular product in mind already, or would you like to see our entire range?'

You get the idea. Your prospect's answer will show you whether that person has something definite in mind, just wants to know more, is just looking, is in a hurry, or is seriously shopping.

In retail, showroom, or door-to-door selling, if a prospect just wants to look around, stay in the background. Stay relaxed but alert. If you show signs of tension, the prospect will sense it and feel pressured. Watch the prospect's body language for clues to his or her interest. Once a prospect lingers for any time over a particular product in your case, display in your shop, or model in your showroom, you have the opportunity to move in and ask if the prospect would like to see something more closely or has any questions about the item.

Once you can get the prospect involved in a dialogue with you, you can ask questions to uncover needs, desires and objections. Questions are a powerful selling tool. Tom Hopkins, the famous American sales trainer, has a saying that explains exactly why questions are so powerful: 'If *you* say it, it's open to doubt. If the *prospect* says it, *it's the truth.*'

Your purpose is to get prospects to tell you their truths — even when you are asking structured questions where you control the choices of answer. Prospects will either choose one of the alternatives you have presented or offer another alternative that gives you the information you need.

Some examples of structured questions:

(a) Are you shopping for yourself, or looking for a gift for someone else?
(b) Would you prefer to look at line X or line Y?
(c) Are you more interested in service A or service B?

If prospects really don't know what they want, use unstructured or open-ended questions to uncover their feelings and needs. Some examples of unstructured questions:

(a) How much were you thinking of investing in this type of product (or service)?
(b) What kind of designs do you prefer?
(c) What kind of functions would you want your machine to perform?

Prospects asked this type of question will often think out loud for you, pre-qualifying themselves and giving you clues to selecting the exact product or service they need.

Use questions to build agreement all the way through the selling process. An agreement question is usually based on something the prospect has already said, either about the product or service you offer, or about his or her own needs. Agreement questions should be phrased so that after the prospect agrees with them, you can build on them. They are your opportunity to introduce additional features or benefits in terms of what they offer the prospect, such as:

(a) You mentioned that your husband wanted a watch that is both shatterproof and waterproof so he can wear it when he's skin-diving, is that correct?
(b) You want a machine that will help your staff get the work done faster, don't you?
(c) Didn't you mention that you wanted one-day service on your typing jobs?

Another useful question to know is the kind used to handle objections. These questions should first restate the objection in question form. That way you will know you are clear about what the objection is. The prospect will also feel that the objection has been acknowledged, heard, and understood (though *not* agreed with). Once you know the objection, you can handle it according to the prospect's response to your question. Some examples of objection questions:

(a) You feel the product would be difficult to use?
(b) You aren't sure the colour matches?

The best way to show you how questions can work is to take you through a sample sequence. For this example, let's say you are a jeweller, and a prospect comes in to look at gold chains. The prospect, whom we'll call Mrs Jones, is strongly attracted to a particular chain, but expresses an objection to the clasp style. You know from experience that this kind of objection is often a cover-up for the real objection (which may be price). But in order to get to that real objection, you have to handle the smaller one first. The dialogue might go like this:

Mrs Jones: 'I really like that chain, but the clasp doesn't look very secure and it looks hard to close.'

You: 'You feel the clasp would be hard to close and would open too easily?'

Mrs Jones: 'That's what it looks like to me.'

You: 'I could easily arrange to have another clasp installed on this chain. It would only take a few moments. Here are two other styles of clasp we could use. Would you prefer this style, or this style?'

At this point, Mrs Jones will either choose one of the clasps, or bring up her real objection. If Mrs Jones chooses, she owns the chain. You could then close with a question like, 'Would you prefer to wait while I change the clasp, or would like to come back to pick up the chain a bit later?' Any remaining hesitation at this point would show that there is still some question, objection, or reason not to buy that must be uncovered and handled. Ask an open-ended question to bring it to light. You could ask something like, 'Is there anything else you need to know about this chain, Mrs Jones?'

Whenever you ask a prospect a question, *listen*. You need the prospect's answers to guide you to the sale. The prospect will often give you opportunities to close the sale sooner than you think. *Listen for them*. Don't talk yourself out of a sale.

10 Direct selling techniques that work

In any type of selling, from retail or industrial to door-to-door or service sales, make sure you always do the following:

1. Have all the materials you need on hand to bring the prospect and the sale together
Keep all your order forms, sales slips, purchase orders, selling materials, and specification sheets organised and ready to use in or near all the places you are likely to be. Have sets in your car, your briefcase, overnight bag, and your desk or counter. Include any advertising reprints, brochures, testimonials or other give-aways that can help you make the sale.

2. Stay well organised so you can find support material quickly
Have the answers handy to questions prospects ask most frequently, so you can find them as you need them. Fumbling around or looking disorganised can lose you the prospect's trust, interest, attention — and the sale. Keep a calculator on hand if you have to do selling arithmetic. It looks accurate and professional, and it's fast.

3. Use testimonials if you have them
Satisfied local customers, especially in industrial, service, consultancy, door-to-door, mail-order, and wholesale selling, can be a most effective sales tool. If you can show a prospect that you have solved someone else's problem with your product or service, your prospect is more likely to trust you with a similar problem or opportunity.

4. Keep your materials fresh
Protect your visual aids, catalogues, and other materials so that they always look tidy and effective. It is part of the overall professional image you are presenting to the prospect.

5. Involve your prospect when you must fill in forms
Know every step and detail of your order form or sales agreement so well that you can keep the prospect interested as you fill it in. Ask questions, reinforce your main selling points, or even get the prospect to assist you in some way. Don't give the prospect too much silent time in which to reconsider. If you have sold honestly, the prospect has made a good decision. Practise this until you can fill in even your most complicated forms almost by heart.

6. Close only if it is a good deal for your prospect
That's right. Salesmanship is *not* the art of manipulating people into making bad decisions, conning someone, or getting them to buy products or services they don't need or can't afford. Nor is it pushing poor service, shoddy products or sloppy workmanship.

A good sale is an act of caring and trust. It involves real regard for your prospect's needs and conditions. If the sale doesn't work for your prospect, it doesn't work for you either. You may get their money once, but you'll never get it again. Greedy salespeople run out of prospects remarkably soon once the word gets around — and it does.

7. Ask for the order when you know it's right
Don't talk around your sale. Ask the customer to act, to buy, to secure and *own* all those benefits the product or service offers.

8. Sell directly related products or services to
   satisfied customers
Wherever you can, use the opportunity of a satisfactory sale to sell related products or services. A few examples will show how you can use this sell-up technique:

(a) Frank has just sold Ron a new, improved paint roller for Ron's do-it-yourself projects. Ron immediately becomes a prospect for paints, paint trays, dust sheets, paint thinners and removers, sandpaper, a new stepladder, and related project supplies.
(b) Paul has just designed a letterhead for a new client, who is delighted with the job. Paul can probably sell that client business cards, brochures, direct mail pieces, catalogues, binders for sales kits etc.

(c) Francis has just sold Jean a beautiful new suit. Jean is now a prime prospect for one or two new blouses, a pair of matching slacks, scarves, belts and accessories, possibly a hat and shoes, a handbag, and maybe a tee shirt or two.

(d) Margaret has just sold her first feature story to a women's magazine editor. Since the editor now knows and likes Margaret's work, that editor becomes a prime prospect for further articles on appropriate topics for women.

9. Look for other clients with related needs

Once you've made one sale to a particular type of customer or business, you have all the facts and techniques you need to sell to anyone else who is in that field. A few examples:

(a) Tony just signed his first contract to supply a local contractor with all the plumbing throughout a brand new housing development. He can now approach other contractors offering the same time, cost and quality benefits, plus fast delivery, that appealed to the first contractor.

(b) Mary sold one customer-designed wall hanging kit to a prominent member of the local gardening club. She could then approach other gardening club members with other craft projects featuring floral motifs.

(c) When Peter finished a spectacular garden landscaping project in a wealthy suburb, he dropped brochures with his business cards into all the houses on the street. The neighbours are now coming to Peter to get the benefit of his talent.

10. Serve your customers once you have sold to them

Take every opportunity to serve your customers after you have made the sale. If your product or service lends itself to educational advertising, or how-to-do-it booklets, or tips for success newsletters, use them to provide a service that reminds customers of you.

Free demonstrations, discounts, gifts, or other special offers can be used to stimulate repeat business. You are offering your customers extra service, which will make them more likely to buy from you next time around.

Using your telephone to get sales

Apart from face-to-face sales, your next most effective tool is the telephone. The telephone is a powerful and personal selling tool that is too often overlooked by small business owners.

When you do direct mailing or advertising, response is increased if you can offer a 24-hour answering service or a freefone number. See that details are given in your ads and mailing shots.

You can use the telephone at any stage of your selling-cycle. Introduce yourself to people who have never heard of you by phone. Pre-qualify prospects by phone. Introduce salespeople to prospects by phone. Follow up your advertising or sales promotion by phone to key prospects and known customers.

Make appointments by telephone. Confirm whether prospects have received your literature. In some cases, you can even get commitments to buy by phone, which can then be followed up in person.

The more telephone calls you make, the more action and interest you are likely to get. Don't be discouraged if a lot of people turn you down. Just go on to the next call, until you line up enough appointments, leads or sales to meet your objectives.

An important point to remember is that calls must be kept brief and interesting. You can only keep a prospect's attention for about eight minutes, unless they know you well (or unless they are the types who like to tell you stories and waste your time on the phone). You should be able to get your main message across and determine whether the prospect would be interested in your offering within those eight minutes.

The rest of this chapter gives you techniques and ideas to assist you in getting the best possible results from your telephone calls. At the end of the chapter, you will find worksheets that can help you design more effective scripts and selling questions for both your face-to-face and telephone sales presentations.

Effective prospecting calls

An effective prospecting call — one that aims to get leads or appointments with potential customers — breaks down into four major components:

1. Introducing yourself, with or without referral information
2. Pre-qualifying the prospect to determine needs
3. Presenting enough information to get the prospect interested or involved

4. Closing by either making the sale, making an appointment, getting a time to phone back, or thanking the prospect and going on to the next call.

These four steps will be discussed fully in this next section.

When prospecting by telephone with people who don't know you or your business, you are likely to average around one in 10 successful calls, depending on the general interest in your type of product or service. With carefully-selected lists of known prospects or buyers, you can do much better than that. The more selective and qualified your phone list, the more interest you are likely to generate.

Many business owners are unjustifiably nervous about using the telephone to get new business or line up appointments with people they don't know personally. They feel that telephone prospecting is an intrusion. Some are shy about calling total strangers.

Don't let that kind of shyness cost you sales. If your product and service have value and fill the needs or desires of your prospects, they'll be glad to hear from you. If the prospect isn't interested, you can always move along quickly without bothering that person further. It will take you only a few moments to find out whether you have a potential sale.

We mentioned earlier that a good prospecting call has four components. Though we shall break them down here for the purposes of analysis, these components should all flow together in your calls. The introduction should lead naturally into the pre-qualifying questions. That, in turn, leads you into the short presentation of interest-building points — if the prospect is qualified. If not, you thank the prospect and move on to the next call.

As mentioned, most calls should not last longer than eight minutes. Unless the customer asks for additional information on the spot, you can usually lead him or her gently into making an appointment with you or your representative.

You don't need to give a lot of detail over the telephone. The point is to give just enough so that the customer will want to see someone for further discussion. Of course, if a prospect expresses immediate willingness to buy over the telephone, you can take down all the information required, then post or deliver the product and invoice afterwards.

To get an idea of how a prospecting call can work, take the case of Norman, who runs an exclusive men's tailoring shop specialising in suits and accessories for executives. He has two telephone lists to work from. One list is cold calls, people who have never heard of him, whose names he has picked up from appointments notices and news items in his local papers. The other list is a referrals list of names of executive men given to him by his own customers, who have also given Norman permission to use their names in his calls.

By comparing the two approaches, referrals and cold calls, you can see how each type of call can be handled for best results. You'll also notice that, though the introduction changes according to the list source, the body of the call remains basically the same.

1. The introduction sets the tone
Your first few seconds on the phone will set up the tone for the whole call. Having a pleasant voice and manner is critical here, as is getting your first identification across clearly and concisely.

On cold calls, here is how Norman introduced himself:

'Good morning, Mr Soandso. I'm Norman T of Executive Tailors Limited. I noticed your appointment in the paper yesterday, and wondered if you would be interested in our Executive Club tailoring service for well-dressed, prominent men. Are you currently having your suits and shirts made to measure, Mr Soandso?'

Notice that Norman introduced his company, told where he had seen the prospect's name, flattered the prospect by referring to him as a well-dressed, prominent man, then led smoothly right into the first pre-qualifying question.

If the prospect then says he doesn't use a tailor, Norman can present and offer his services on the grounds that the man is obviously smart and aggressive enough to be promoted, therefore a made-to-measure wardrobe would add credibility and visibility to the man's image.

If the prospect does use a tailor, Norman can find out whether he is satisfied with his current tailor, what items he has his tailor make for him, and whether the prospect would be interested in his made-to-measure range of shirts and accessories.

If the prospect says he's simply not interested, Norman can do one more of three things:

(a) He can say 'thank you very much' and go on to the next call.

(b) He can find out when the prospect is likely to be interested and get a date to phone back.
(c) He can offer to send the prospect his brochure outlining all Norman's services, 'just in case'.

A combination of the last two is the most logical approach. Norman does send out the brochures — which are elegantly designed and show both the clothing ranges and alteration services — whether the prospect expresses interest or not.

Here is Norman's introduction to referral calls:

'Good morning, Mr Soandso. I'm Norman T of Executive Tailors Limited. Charles S (Norman's customer) recommended that I phone you about our new range of hand-finished, made-to-measure business shirts. He thought you might be interested because he considers you have such good taste in clothes. Are you currently having your clothes tailored, Mr Soandso?'

On paper, this approach may seem like blatant flattery, but with the right tone of sincerity, it definitely gets the prospect's attention. Make sure your own customers are the type of referrals from whom this would sound like a compliment. Again, the opening leads right into the pre-qualification questions.

2. Pre-qualifying customers
To continue with Norman as an example, here are some of the other pre-qualifying questions that he might ask once the prospect expresses interest.

'Could you tell me your regular suit size in off-the-peg clothes, Mr Soandso?' Norman knows enough about body sizes to appreciate what fitting problems the man has from knowing his suit size, and can follow up with another question. If, for example, the man answered, 'I wear a 44 length', which is a large size, Norman could ask, 'Do you find that you have trouble with the fit of your jacket sleeves, or the proportions of the trousers in your off-the-peg suits?' If a man answers in a size that Norman knows is short, he can ask something like, 'Do you find that ready-to-wear suits don't really show off your proportions to advantage?'

Norman's questions are designed to get agreement from the prospect and at the same time point out disadvantages of not having clothes tailored. In pre-qualifying, the point is to get a series of agreements from prospects that will show his or her need and lead you naturally to the close — which is giving the prospect the opportunity to fill that need with your products or services.

A few more questions that Norman uses show how to get the prospect involved in pre-qualifying him or herself:

'Wouldn't you feel more comfortable in clothes that are made-to-measure for you, so they fit well and show you off to advantage, Mr Soandso?'

'If you could get a hand-finished made-to-measure shirt designed *for you* at a price no higher than you'd pay at more exclusive men's outfitters, wouldn't you be interested, Mr Soandso?'

'If I could offer you a hand-finished made-to-measure sports jacket (or whatever) in your choice of the best materials, would it fit in with your current wardrobe needs, Mr Soandso?'

'If you could get a 10 per cent discount on our exclusive accessories, plus free alterations to two suits in your current wardrobe, would you be interested in joining our Executive Club, Mr Soandso?'

3. Handling objections

Of course, a prospect can make an objection at any stage of your call. If you hear something like, 'I'd like that, but I can't afford it now', or 'I don't think I'm ready for that yet', *welcome that objection.* It means the customer is interested enough to get involved. You then have the opportunity to find out if the objection is just resistance from having been caught off-guard (in which case it can probably be overcome) or a real block to the sale.

When a prospect comes up with an objection, ask a question that can either clarify it or eliminate it. Let's say a prospect says he can't afford a new suit or jacket right now. Norman could say any of these things in reply:

'Would it make you more comfortable, Mr Soandso, if I told you that we have three different payment plans that allow you to choose the amount you'd like to invest in your clothes each month?'

'I'm not asking you to buy anything right away, Mr Soandso. I would much rather you come into our showroom and see the quality and style of our work before you make any wardrobe investments. Would you be able to take half an hour on Thursday evening just to come and look around?'

'I believe our Executive Club prices on such quality

workmanship are much lower than you would expect, Mr Soandso. Do you feel that £25 a month would be too much to invest in a suit that will last for as long as you enjoy wearing it?'

'When you consider that one of our classic business suits will probably be a mainstay of your business wardrobe for at least five years, the investment isn't that much. Are you more interested in the original cost or the overall long-term value, Mr Soandso?'

Treat an objection as an opportunity to stress another customer benefit, once you have listened to and handled the objection. Make sure you phrase your own questions in ways that don't invite the customer to say no. If the customer does come up with a real and undeniable block to the sale, thank him, end the call, and move on. You'll find other prospects who will honestly benefit from your product or service, so there's no need to bother anyone who can't buy.

In cases like that, however, it is still a good idea to send out your promotional literature with your card.

4. Presenting your product or service

You don't always need to do much telephone presenting. In some cases, the prospect will get involved enough for you to move right to the 'close', that is, making an appointment with the prospect. In Norman's case, his objective was to get prospects into his showroom. He felt that once they were on his premises, the quality and style of both the materials and the finished clothes would do most of the selling for him.

Your own product or service may need to be demonstrated to prospects in their own offices or homes. In a case like that, or where your service or product needs some explaining to get the prospect more interested, telephone presentation can really help.

Stress the benefits to the customer on the telephone just the way you would in your advertising. (Review Chapter 1 to analyse the benefits of your product or service.) You don't need to say much. You can get your two or three major benefits across quickly, so the prospect can decide whether he or she wants to know more in person.

Taking Norman's example, here are a few benefit statements you could adapt.

'We guarantee that you'll get the kind of perfect fit and hand finishing that makes you look as professional as you are, yet feel completely comfortable at the same time.'

'Your choice of fine and exclusive fabrics means you get a unique, elegant suit that's designed only for you. You won't see your suit on all the junior executives in your firm.'

'You'll look both fashionable and elegant in one of our suits, Mr Soandso. We tailor our designs to bring out the best in your own proportions.'

If the prospect expresses interest in one of your benefit statements, you can then try for the close. You may have to do two or three trial closes before the prospect either agrees to an appointment or says a definite no. In each case, you can handle the objection as outlined above, then go for a close again.

5. The close is some form of commitment

Whether you want a sale, an appointment, a chance to send literature, or even just a time to call back, your close involves getting some form of commitment and involvement from the prospect.

Give the prospect choices, so he or she doesn't have to say 'no'. You can try one of these approaches, adapted to your business:

'Would Wednesday or Thursday be a better day for you to see me, Mr Soandso?'

'Do you find it more convenient to discuss this kind of service over lunch, or in the morning?'

'Would you be able to drop by on our late night, or would you prefer to come in during the weekend?'

'I'd like to set up a special showing just for you, Mr Soandso. Would you prefer to see our new lines on Wednesday or Thursday?'

'Would you rather I come to see you in person, or would you like to see our product literature first, Mr Soandso?'

If the prospect still says no, but seems sympathetic, you could try to get referral names. You can say something like, 'I'm sorry you can't use our new service right now, Mr Soandso, but would you be kind enough to share the names with me of two of your colleagues who might be interested?' Again, if he or she says no to that, accept it gracefully and move on.

6. Always thank the prospect

No matter whether the prospect agrees to see you or buy from you, always thank the prospect for his or her time. If you remain courteous and polite, even when the prospect says no, that prospect will remember you favourably.

A prospect who says no now could be in the market in six months. If you have impressed him or her, you may get the business at that point. But you won't if you are rude or brusque, or get upset when the prospect says no.

Using a telephone script

You may feel more comfortable using a telephone script that you have written out before your call. A telephone script can help you organise your thoughts so you don't miss any of the major points you wish to convey. You can write or type your selling/prospecting sequence on one or two sheets of paper.

Another technique is to use a separate file card to write out each point. Label each card with key phrases at the top, so you can spot benefits and selling points quickly as you talk.

In either format, organise your sales sequence in the order in which you would present your points in person. Don't get stuck in your script or let a script prevent you from listening to your customer or prospect. A script should be a guide for you. Your customer's responses will show you what points to cover next. Try to keep your tone natural and flowing, whether or not you use a script. The sample script on page 68 is a simple example which you can adapt to your own business needs. (See page 71 for a worksheet that will help you write your own.) This one is a telephone script for a service company that can be adapted to generate leads and appointments, especially for service businesses.

10 Tips for more effective telephone use

Whenever you use your telephone, you reflect your business style and your own personality by the way in which you use it. You're making contact with others on a powerful and personal medium.

Too many people in business tend to abuse and misuse the telephone. It is not a tool for venting emotions, interrupting people unnecessarily, or wasting valuable business time on personal problems.

Effective telephone use is a combination of good business manners and efficiency. When you're using the phone to back up personal contact or post, you're being granted another opportunity to make a sale.

TELEPHONE SCRIPT
Personnel Management Associates

'Good morning. Is (*executive's name*) in?'

If yes: go to A when prospect comes on phone.

If no: get a time to call back and record it.

If asked who is calling:

'It's (*your name*) from Personnel Management. I wrote to (*executive*) recently and just need a few moments of his time. Is he in, please?'

A. 'Good morning (*prospect name*). I'm (*your name*) from Personnel Management Associates, the sales and marketing recruitment specialists. Did you receive the letter I wrote to you last week?'

If yes: go to **B.**

If no, or 'what's it about?':

'In my letter I was introducing myself and our company's services for the times when you're looking for qualified sales or marketing people. I specialise in the (*name of industry*) industry, because of my own experience in your field.'

B. 'Does your company plan to hire any new marketing or sales people within the next six months?'

If yes, go to **C.**

If no, or 'don't know':

'Fine (*prospect name*). When would be the best time to call you again to see if Personnel Management Associates could be of assistance in finding good people for you?' Get and record callback date. Go to **D.**

If prospect says, 'I don't deal with that':

'Fine (*prospect name*). Could you please tell me who does?' Get name and check spelling; then: 'What is the best time to call (*name*), do you know?' Get callback time and go to **D.**

C. 'I'd like to make an appointment with you at your convenience — to discuss whether I could be of assistance in your personnel recruiting. Is (*date, eg, Wednesday*) or (*Thursday*) better for you, (*prospect*)?' Choose two dates when you want to see prospect. If prospect chooses date, set appointment time and go to **E.** If prospect refuses your two dates *but* sets another, get time and go to **E.** If prospect says, 'I can't see you *now*', get callback time and go to **D.** If prospect says, 'We don't need you', or 'We do our own', go to **D.**

D. 'Thank you very much for your time (*name*). Good day.'

E. 'Thanks for your time (*prospect*). I look forward to meeting you on (*appointment date*).'

If customers telephone you to complain about your products or services, treat that as a chance to keep a valued customer. Don't get angry, or rude, or hang up on them. After all, they have given *you* the first crack at solving their problems, rather than silently going off and buying from your competitor.

Here, then, are 10 tips to make telephone contacts more rewarding for you.

1. Always use good telephone manners

No matter how upset you get, stay pleasant and calm on the telephone. Get the caller's name, so you can use it in conversation. Be polite at all times. Don't shout near the phone, or keep the customer holding on too long. When you have to transfer a call to a member of staff make sure you introduce that person clearly, so the customer knows who he or she is talking to. Treat callers as you would like to be treated.

2. Make sure staff identify themselves clearly on the phone

Customers and suppliers like to know who they're dealing with. Have your staff practise answering the phone with your shop or business name, then their own name, then 'May I help you?' Staff with difficult names to pronounce or remember should be especially careful about speaking clearly and distinctly when they answer the telephone.

3. Never mumble or mutter on the phone

Speak slowly, clearly, and distinctly. Go over details more than once if they aren't understood the first time. You can speak clearly without being too loud. People need to hear you, but don't like being addressed in a loud manner. If you tend to speak very fast, slow down. People take a bit longer to register what you're saying when they can't see your face. Pause occasionally, so the customer can respond.

4. A good telephone voice can be a real asset in business

If you tend to speak in a monotone, work to develop a more pleasing telephone voice. Smile while you are talking, and convey that smile with your voice. High-pitched or squeaky voices, nasal tones, and dull voices tend to turn people off on the phone. Listen to yourself on a tape recorder, and work to open up and deepen your voice, as well as varying your vocal range. We've found that our own telephone voice helps people to remember us. We do our best to make that vocal memory a pleasant one.

5. Have your secretary dial calls to save time
When you're trying to reach busy executives, your secretary can save you time by dialling your calls for you. Be ready to pick up the phone yourself as soon as the other party is on the phone. Don't use this technique to keep people waiting, or show them how important you are — it's strictly a time-saver.

6. Set definite telephone hours for staff, supplier or
   customer problems
Whether it's between 9 and 11 am or 3 to 5 pm, set up a specific time for telephone work and problem-solving, then let everyone know about it. If people call outside these hours, have your staff take their numbers and let them know your times for returning calls. If you and your staff handle it properly, customers won't be offended, and you'll have other blocks of uninterrupted time during the day for work and selling.

7. Have all relevant material organised for your
   phone calls beforehand
Memos, reports, purchase orders, delivery slips and notes from previous phone conversations should all be right in front of you before you get on the phone. Having your facts organised and at your fingertips will save you valuable telephone time. Make an agenda for each call outlining the topics you want to cover, so you take care of each point. A few key phrases written down will help ensure that you stay on track.

8. Use telephone number sheets when you're banking calls
Take five minutes at the end of one day to organise the next day's telephone call list. Write down the numbers, contact names, and reason for calling on one sheet. Then you can run through all your calls at once, quickly and completely. Leave enough space on your phone list to make notes of action to be taken, decisions made, or anything else you need to know to follow up each call.

9. Keep conversations as short as possible to get the job done
Unless the problems or tasks you're facing are complex, your telephone time doesn't need to be long for each call. If you're well-organised, you should be able to get through the business at hand in under five minutes. You don't need a lot of time spent on small talk to do business. A few short friendly remarks will cover the social aspects — then get to business.

10. *Substitute conference calls for meetings whenever you can*

If you need to talk with two or three people in different offices, whether in the same city or different cities, conference calls can be a real time-saver. It's much faster to use a phone link-up than to get people together physically. You save travel time and often save meeting time, too. If everyone has an agenda for the conference call, and is properly prepared, you'll probably cut your time in half. Costs for this service are likely to fall as its use increases; it is being actively promoted by British Telecom.

The following worksheet is to help you write your own personal contact and telephone scripts.

PERSONAL AND TELEPHONE SELLING WORKSHEET

1. Make up five introductory alternative-choice questions you could ask when a prospect first walks in or contacts you.

2. Make up three *structured* questions that you could ask prospects to get information.

3. Make up three *open-ended* questions that would get prospects to express what they want from your business.

4. Make up five *agreement* questions you could use to introduce new features and benefits to your prospects, once they agree.

5. Make up two questions that restate prospect *objections*.

6. Make up 10 specific *benefit statements* that you could use either in person or on the telephone:

7. Make up five alternative-choice *closing* questions that you could use to get some form of commitment from the prospect.

8. Write out the introduction to yourself and your business that you would use for a telephone script.

9. Write out three pre-qualifying questions you could ask prospects in a telephone script.

10. Write out three closing questions you could or would ask prospects in a telephone script.

11. Checklist of 20 telephone business-builders you can use. Go through this list and tick all the ways you could use your telephone to build new sales for *your* business.

    1. ☐ Introduce myself to new customers
    2. ☐ Sell new lines or services to current customers
    3. ☐ Pre-qualify unknown prospects
    4. ☐ Generate leads and referrals

5. ☐ Do fast research on new market potential
6. ☐ Remind customers of other products or services I have
7. ☐ Get customer reaction to upcoming business plans
8. ☐ Confirm order details, terms, delivery dates
9. ☐ Reconfirm sales appointments, or make them
10. ☐ Remind customers of the convenience of dealing with my business
11. ☐ Handle customer complaints and problems quickly
12. ☐ Revitalise dormant accounts
13. ☐ Precede or follow up mailing shots or personal calls
14. ☐ Sell products or service on a trial basis
15. ☐ Extra-personal promotion of special events and sales
16. ☐ Find new suppliers or compare supplier prices and services
17. ☐ Supplement credit and collection letters
18. ☐ Get credit information and updates faster
19. ☐ Promote my own local credit
20. ☐ Invite customers or prospects in for an introductory cup of coffee.

Chapter 4

Using Free Publicity, Local Community Groups and Public Relations to Make Yourself Known

This chapter and Chapters 5 to 7 are about the techniques which you can use to take your own sales campaign out into the world faster than you could door to door. These methods include using public relations and free publicity, covered in this chapter; sales promotion and direct mailing, covered in Chapter 5; general advertising, covered in Chapter 6 and cooperative advertising, covered in Chapter 7.

When you use any one of these methods, you are increasing your impact on the market place. You are reaching out to bring prospective customers in, rather than sitting back and waiting for them to come to you.

Consider any funds that you put into these selling methods as investments in your future business, rather than as expenses (except for tax purposes, of course). You may use only one of these techniques at any time or a combination of three or four during your business year. The various methods are included so that you are *aware* of the alternatives open to you, and can choose those that are the most appropriate for your business and your budget.

If you are just starting up and have limited funds, you can begin by trying to get free publicity from your local newspapers, free weekly advertising journals, radio and early evening local television programmes. Local community centres or groups are a fertile source of free publicity, and some ideas are presented in this chapter.

Once you are better established and more solvent, you can afford to do inexpensive leaflets or direct mailing, reinforced by the occasional classified ad or short-time advertising.

Your annual advertising campaigns and large-scale sales promotions can be expanded once your income has grown sufficiently to warrant it. Of course, even in the absence of increased income, loans may permit this.

How local community groups and customer/public relations can help you sell

One of the most important areas of sales relations is the interaction your company has with various groups in the general public. It is not only your relationship with your own customers and prospective customers, but your standing in the local community which is important.

A customer/public relations and local community group campaign, no matter how effective, is no substitute for quality merchandise or service, knowledgeable and polite staff, competitive prices and a convenient location. But good public relations can keep present customers coming back to you, and often attract new customers by word of mouth.

In this age of increasing automation, people still appreciate the old-fashioned values of personal service, and your involvement with them and the community. This is enhanced by your giving the best possible service or products to your customers.

Community public relations can spread that personal touch and image of involvement into the community at large for your business. It can build up good relationships with key buying influences before you even call on them. Your customers and community relations programmes can give you a competitive edge with the consuming public.

By getting involved with good causes and supporting your community, you are giving back value to the people who have supported you — your friends, neighbours and customers. Also as this next section will show, you can also create opportunities to build more community awareness of your business, which can lead to more sales for you.

Take special note of the tips and examples on preparing good publicity releases and materials for editorial use in your local media. Use them to ensure that you get the press coverage you want when you are working in the community.

25 Ways to use community service public relations to build sales

Community service public relations is a very special way to become more active as a part of your local community. You won't always achieve an immediate payoff in increased sales or shop traffic. You won't always be able to write off all your costs. You will, however, gain in local goodwill, and you will have the satisfaction of creating something worthwhile for your community that cannot be measured in cash terms.

At the same time, you don't have to be an anonymous donor. You can do something good *and* get the maximum publicity value for your business, which can lead eventually to more sales and other long-term financial benefits. Don't forget that many of the real business leaders in your community became leaders by contributing service to the community. Join them, work with them to improve the local quality of life, and you will be amazed at how many profitable opportunities can open up for your business.

After reading through this selection of community service ideas, you will find tips and checklists to help you prepare appropriate and usable publicity releases and materials for your projects.

The amount of news or media cooperation you get will depend on the news or feature value that an editor or programme director sees in your project. Your publicity releases and public service announcements must convey those values. Both the format and the content of your material should make it as easy as possible for the press to use your news. The second half of this chapter shows you how.

1. Donate to local causes
Donate money, new or used supplies, equipment, products or services that you sell to a needy school, youth group or local charity.

2. Sponsor a collection for children in need
Collect from your customers and prospects sporting goods, clothes, games, and toys no longer in use. Give them to a charity organisation for redistribution to needy children or resale in a charity shop. You could offer small gifts or discounts for a limited period to those who bring in goods.

3. Trade-ins to make gifts
Approach schools and institutions, clubs or teams with special trade-in offers on new products or equipment in return for their older equipment. Donate those trade-ins to your local community or arts centre.

4. Promote free events for disabled people
Sponsor a series of films, demonstrations or field trips for the handicapped, or for other disadvantaged groups.

5. Teach young people about business
Set up a course to teach teenagers about retailing, business management or other topics that tie in with your business. Work through the schools.

6. Set up a career day
Work with the local Chamber of Commerce or careers officers in schools to set up a Careers Day with talks and exhibits.

7. Do a youth training programme
Set up a part-time course in your business for older local students or participate in the Youth Training Scheme. Your trainees could also become reliable part-time and summer workers in your business as a result.

8. Sponsor a sports team
Sponsoring a youth or adult team has publicity value. Create a team of your own in some sport. Join a group that works with children in need. Put your money where the real need is.

9. Form a young peoples' business group
Form and lead a Young People's Business Group in cooperation with your local Boy Scouts and Girl Guides, Chamber of Commerce, or a local church or school. Invite interesting speakers on different aspects of local business, such as local bankers, manufacturers, or service industries in your area. Groups can also do projects that will help them understand how business works in your community. If you need extra ideas for projects, talk to the business studies teachers at your local schools or colleges.

10. Send needy children on a summer holiday
Set up a scheme to send one or more children whose parents couldn't otherwise afford it, on a summer holiday. Your social services department can provide you with appropriate candidates. This is one area where you can get your own customers involved in your worthy cause for extra goodwill.

Set up a display with a donation box explaining your scheme, and ask for contributions. Put a special section in your regular advertising about your summer holiday sponsorship. Enlist the support of your local newspaper in getting editorial coverage for the projects.

You can set a financial target that includes all accommodation and transport fees plus a small amount of spending money for each child. Include a selection of appropriate holiday clothes and shoes.

11. Start a club
Start a sports or fitness club for youngsters or adults (or both), with tee shirts, their own newsletter, and arrangements at a local gym or fitness club for special volume discount prices. You can also organise a year-round programme of demonstrations, speakers, films, field trips or sporting/fitness events and competitions. Promote values of good sportsmanship, safety, good health and fair play.

Start a club that fits in with some aspect of your business. Look for ways to tie in your business with community problems and opportunities, or education.

12. Set up regular classes
You could also sponsor classes on topics relating to business or sales or management, as well as good business practices. Approach your local schools, colleges, or adult education night schools. Enlist the cooperation of teachers. Tailor the subject matter to the group you want to reach.

13. Encourage youth involvement in local government
Choose one teenage delegate from each of your local secondary schools, to work with your business to teach and promote good citizenship to their contemporaries and to younger children. Your youthful 'board' can also sponsor awards of cash or merchandise to outstanding local students, as well as encourage teenage participation in community projects. Find out from your town hall or other local officials what projects around town could be handled by teenage volunteers.

14. Set up a scholarship
Set up a scholarship for one student a year. You could either collect nominations from local teachers or get nominations at your place of business to generate customer interest. Once the nominations with the candidates' qualifications are in, you can either have a panel decide the award, or throw it open to

a vote by ballot on your premises. The scholarship can be given on a basis of academic achievement, participation in extra-curricular activities, service to the community (through church or school or service groups) and overall good character.

15. Support a handicapped team
The recent success of sporting events and olympics for the handicapped suggests another area where you could make a real contribution. You could sponsor a handicapped team, donate equipment, teach classes for the handicapped, and cooperate with the local organisations for the handicapped in their programmes. Ask around to find out where the real needs are.

16. Develop work schemes for handicapped people
If there are homes or special shelters for the handicapped in your area, help them develop skill-teaching courses, and donate the necessary time, money or equipment.

17. Organise a benefit
Sponsor a dance, raffle, sports contest or film festival, with proceeds to benefit the handicapped.

18. Sponsor a clean-up day
Get teenagers involved in cleaning up any litter or eyesores in your community. Work with the local schools and parks departments. Include a party or dance for participants later, and try to arrange for free food and drink in local fast-food chains in return for publicity. Get special anti-litter, painting and clean-up teams organised to blitz local parks, clear up ugly spots, and plant flowers or trees in public rest areas under supervision. You can probably get newspaper coverage both before the day and on the day itself. Generate extra interest by encouraging competition between schools or teams, with suitable prizes for everyone.

19. Don't forget senior citizens
Many senior citizens have the time, money and health to truly enjoy their retirement, and they have a thirst for information and activities that will help them stay involved and fit. Start your own Golden Age Club, with special discounts from your own and other local businesses. Offer them films, speakers, and courses designed to help them make the most out of their retirement years.

20. *Set up a mobile shopping service for people confined to the home*

Use a mobile shop with a door-to-door salesperson. Work from lists given to you by local churches and social service departments. Use the telephone to contact prospects to offer them the opportunity to buy from you at home.

21. *Join as many groups as you have time for*

Join and be active in one or more local service groups, such as the Round Table or Rotary. You will make good personal contacts who may become customers as well as friends. You will also find out where your contributions would do the most good in your community.

22. *Use local labour*

Use local labour and sources of supply as much as possible, especially for your own business needs, such as making signs, preparing advertising, hiring staff, and buying office supplies, fixtures, and lighting. Your suppliers could become your prospects, and they will often tell their friends and colleagues about the work they did for you.

23. *Make your voice heard in local government*

Participate in local government and civic groups. Cooperate with civic officials in meeting community problems. Join any special-interest committees dealing with business problems. Speak out about important local issues that can affect your community life.

24. *Promote local culture*

Promote the educational and cultural life of the community.

25. *Use word of mouth*

Don't overlook the value of local word of mouth, both in enlisting support for your projects and in making them known throughout the community. Talk about your projects wherever you go. If you're excited about your project, let people know about it. Your own enthusiasm will generate interest and support from others, *which often lead to sales.*

Now you know what to do, the next section will show you how to get good business-building publicity while you're doing it.

How to get free publicity for your business

What do you need to do to get the publicity value out of your community service projects? First, be aware of the needs and limitations of all your local media. Remember, each newspaper, radio or TV station is aiming at a particular audience, and wants news or feature material that will be of value to that audience.

Ongoing courses, awards, classes you hold or causes you support are sometimes considered worthy of feature coverage, which is based on human-interest factors. You may be able to get on to a local radio or TV chat show, or have your story reported in the local newspaper.

All the media will be looking for the local interest, names, news angles, or feature angles that make the story a service to readers. For a local newspaper, local names and personalities are very important. The overall community service aspects of the project tend to interest editors on the daily newspapers.

Radio stations allocate a certain amount of their air time to what are called public service announcements. If you're having a class, dance, or other event that will benefit a local charity or youth group, your event might qualify for these free announcements.

Type your radio announcement on one sheet, with the who, what, when, why, and where facts all stated clearly in less than 100 words.

Put your name and phone number for contacts at the top as well as the dates you would like to see the announcement aired (if the event is 1 May, and you want airing or publicity for the previous two weeks, put 'For release 15 April-1 May' at the top).

Television news coverage is ordinarily only on the day of the event, and usually not unless there's some visual activity that will interest viewers.

For both radio and TV, the news director for news coverage and the programme director for feature or announcement coverage are the people to contact. Get their names with a phone call. Then send them your material. They will contact you if they need further information, which is why it's important that your name and phone number be at the top of each release you send.

Short news announcements for your daily and weekly newspapers are handled the same way and sent to the city or sports editors, depending on the nature of the event.

Whatever you do, play it straight with the media. Don't say you're going to produce a big name unless you know for sure you will. If your dates or plans change, let the media know right away. Don't exaggerate the amount of donations or number of participants in a project.

As long as your community service projects involve real service and have honest news or human-interest value, you should have no trouble getting the publicity your effort deserves.

Writing good press releases

Start your release copy with a paragraph that can build reader interest, then state your basic facts. If the news editor or features editor of your newspaper finds your project interesting enough, he or she will probably assign a staff or freelance writer to the story.

The format tips for press releases and photos described below will give you more specific information on organising and sending your releases. What's important for you to keep in mind is that TV and radio generally want shorter releases than newspapers.

See the example of a press release on page 86.

1. Be newsworthy
Make sure first that you have a newsworthy story to tell.

2. Make it easy for an editor to use
Use the inverted pyramid style for both news and feature releases: put the *who, what, when, why* and *where* basic facts in the first or first and second paragraphs of the release. Add background or other facts after those in descending order of importance. This gives the editor a chance to cut the story if necessary without losing the basic facts.

On feature material, start with a sentence or paragraph stressing the human-interest angle first, then back it up immediately after with the five w's mentioned above.

3. Keep it simple
Keep the release as short, simple, direct and clear as possible.

4. Always type
Type all releases on one side of standard size typewriter bond or letterhead paper. If you have two sides of copy, use two

sheets. Always double space, so the editor has room to add or correct copy.

5. Give contact information
Type your name and phone number at the top of each sheet as a contact. Also, put the dates when you prefer the information released right at the top of the sheet.

6. Be accurate
Double check the accuracy of all names, dates, numbers, and facts you use.

7. Know who you're approaching for coverage
Know the names of editors, programme directors or news directors of your local media, who their audiences are, and which aspects of news or feature materials each one covers, so you're sending the right stories to the right places. Keep your mailing lists up to date at all times.

8. Send photos that can be used
Use clear, crisp, good-contrast 5 x 7 or 8 x 10 in glossy black and white photos (unless the editor specifically requests other types of material). Don't send a polaroid or small colour print, colour slides, photocopy of a photo, or any picture that's blurred, too dark or too light. If the picture isn't clear, don't send it.

9. Attach captions carefully
Always attach a caption to every photo you send. Don't use paperclips or staples to attach them, as those will mar the photo. Attach the caption to the back of the photo, and use petroleum based adhesive or tape that will come off without tearing it.

10. Don't mark the photo
Never write on the front of a photo. If you write on the back for identification purposes, use a grease pencil (available from art supply or office equipment shops) that won't leave marks that show on the front.

11. Identify the subjects clearly
Give the name and title of every person in the photo and the order in which they are shown (eg, left to right, clockwise from the top etc).

12. Include the photo with the right story
Send the photo with the release it's supposed to illustrate.

13. Protect photos
Always use a cardboard stiffener when sending a photo. Also write on the outer envelope: 'Photo do not bend!'

14. Use professionals if possible
Hire the best photographer you can, especially for events where you want to get human interest shots and action photos. The photographer should also be able to help you get more interesting group shots, where people seem to be interacting instead of staring into the camera.

15. Keep duplicate photos
Set up a filing system for duplicates of the photos you've sent out and for other background photos on your events. That way, if a photo gets lost, you can supply another one.

16. Stay out of the way in photo sessions
Help photographers line up subjects, but don't interfere.

17. What not to do when sending press releases

(a) Don't mislead the media. That includes distortions and exaggerations.
(b) Don't expect an editor to use a release unless it's news.
(c) Don't ask why a feature, story or photo isn't used.
(d) Don't expect preferential treatment because you're an advertiser. The editor's first duty is to his or her readers, listeners or viewers.
(e) Don't send releases to publishers, ad managers or salespeople.
(f) Don't favour one journal on new releases. On features, alternate between competitive media, so each is getting opportunities for exclusives at regular intervals. Respect exclusives dug up by news writers.
(g) Don't send a release at the very last minute and expect it to be used. If you have material you don't want announced until a certain date, send it ahead of time, and specify the date for release at the top of the first page ('Not to be released until 6 April 1984').
(h) Never send a release without some type of release date on it, where the editor can see it clearly and immediately.

(i) Don't over-use the name of a product or organisation in your copy. Don't use all capital letters for your business or store name, or the name of your project.

(j) Don't send sloppy or poorly written releases to any medium simply because 'you know they'll rewrite them anyway'. They probably won't — instead your material will end up in the waste bin.

(k) Don't blanket newspapers with stories devoid of any local angles.

(l) Don't call up editors or news directors asking if material is going to be used or asking for clippings or air times.

(m) Above all, don't send material for the wrong market to the wrong editor or newsperson in the wrong medium. Check to make sure that your release has specific appeal for that editor talking to that audience in that medium. The little bit of extra work you put in here will be well worth it in terms of increasing your coverage and cooperation from the press.

Two publicity success stories

Mary, a craft shop owner had decided that one of her best prospect groups was older women, including those in senior citizens' homes. She decided to do some of her 'good works' with retired women. She began by donating one evening a week and some inexpensive supplies to teaching craftwork in the local senior citizens' home. Her participants were so enthusiastic about the classes that Mary soon had enough enquiries from relatives and friends to do two more classes a week where people paid for their materials and her time.

She then decided to sponsor a Christmas crafts bazaar at the home, featuring work made by all three of her classes and their friends. The proceeds would be split between the maker of the item and a local church group who worked with less fortunate older people.

Mary sent out press releases and publicity material that was picked up by virtually every local medium. The radio stations used her public service announcements about the bazaar itself. The TV station did a 10-minute mini-documentary on the project and how it was benefiting both the senior citizens doing it and those less fortunate. The women's pages of the local newspaper did an illustrated feature on the quality and originality of the craftwork to be sold in the bazaar.

In every case, Mary's name was mentioned, often with the name of her shop. The extensive press coverage, combined with word of mouth was soon attracting people from a 25-mile radius to buy craft kits and supplies for themselves and as Christmas gifts.

What did Mary send out that got the media so involved? She sent a simple but complete press kit featuring a few photos of her senior students working on projects, a press release/public service announcement (see page 87), and some background material giving in-depth information on the project and what it was intended to accomplish. Both content and presentation followed the format outlined in the checklist in the section on press releases (page 81).

A second case involved Tom, who owns a small leather goods manufacturing company. He also has a real gift and passion for working with mentally handicapped children. He began a vocational training course in leatherwork for these children right in his own factory. The children were assigned different tasks according to their capacities, and they shared equally in the profits.

Tom did not publicise himself. A relative of one of the children worked at a large daily newspaper and told the features editor about Tom's work project. The editor came out to observe, wrote up almost a full page about the project, and took photographs of the children at work.

Tom started getting calls and orders from readers all over the region as soon as the story appeared. Orders for the children's work came in for months after the story as well. In addition, Tom's regular business with local and regional retailers benefited from the media publicity.

SAMPLE PRESS RELEASE

FOR IMMEDIATE RELEASE
USE UP TO 12 NOVEMBER 1984

SENIOR CITIZENS TO HOLD
BENEFIT CRAFT BAZAAR
13 NOVEMBER

1 October 1984
For more information,
contact: Mary Smith
Clever Crafts Unlimited
31 Shady Lane
Phone: 0532 8021

On Saturday 13 November 1984, the residents of the Sunnydale Senior Citizens' Home will hold a Christmas Crafts Bazaar, featuring handmade gifts, toys, household items, wall hangings, rugs, and other work for sale. The Bazaar will open at 10.00 am, and run until all items are sold. Proceeds from the sale will be split between the Sunnydale residents and Age Concern, sponsored by St Simon's Church.

The Bazaar will offer over 400 handcrafted projects designed for Christmas giving and home use. Many are unique items created especially for the bazaar by the senior citizens who have been doing craft projects since January under the guidance of Mary Smith, the home's crafts coordinator. Forty-two of the home's residents have been knitting, crocheting, embroidering, carving, sewing and needlepointing with a goal of raising £3000 to support St Simon's in continuing its Meals on Wheels scheme for elderly people confined to home throughout the community.

Ms Smith, who began teaching craftwork at Sunnydale 18 months ago, explains, 'The senior students came up with the bazaar idea as a way in which they could both enjoy doing the crafts themselves and continue to contribute to the community. They felt that the most appropriate place to donate the proceeds of their work was to other senior citizens less fortunate than themselves. St Simon's scheme looked like the most practical way to support and assist those others.'

Chapter 5

Using Sales Promotion and Direct Mail to Build Your Business

Sales promotion and direct mail are both powerful tools that you can use for meeting short-term business and sales objectives. They are being covered in the same chapter because they are most often (though not always) used together.

Direct mail, along with your media advertising, can be used effectively to inform your key prospects and customers about your sales promotional activities. Direct mail can be one of the most selective advertising techniques, because you choose precisely which people will get your direct mail.

Surveys have shown that direct mail produces the greatest response among the trades and professions. The next best way to reach them is by specially printed inserts in trade magazines and professional journals; some publishers may accept them on a regional basis, but usually, the whole printing must be covered. Local newsagents can sometimes be persuaded to put inserts into local newspaper deliveries; a deal with a few local agents could cover your entire community.

What is sales promotion?

Sales promotion is simply any sales activity that *supplements* personal selling or advertising and helps to make them more effective. It includes special events, demonstrations, promotion kits, displays, theme sales, stock clearance sales, new product promotions or service promotions, and much more.

Sales promotion is out of the ordinary routine of sales efforts. It is the special push you give to promote sales of specific products or services over a short and clearly set period of time. Whatever sales promotion you plan should fit in with your overall marketing plan.

Sales promotion can be used to:

(a) Build up shop traffic or find new clients/customers for your business.

(b) Extend selling seasons on seasonal items and services.
(c) Clear out old or slow-moving stock.
(d) Broaden your business area or customer base.
(e) Meet a specific competitive situation.
(f) Increase the value per order of your sales.
(g) Reclaim lost or dormant accounts.
(h) Introduce new products, lines or services you offer.
(i) Build customer goodwill and involvement in your business.

Direct mail can be used either as part of a sales promotion or on its own to perform the same nine tasks. Both media are designed to bring prospects and customers to you, either in person, by telephone or by mail order.

How to organise a sales promotion

In the next section there are 20 ideas for sales promotions. Each one is designed to help you get your customers and their friends involved with your business and/or build traffic or new business.

Each of these ideas has an inherent news peg that can help you achieve local editorial coverage and more awareness of your business or shop by present and prospective customers.

Most of these ideas can be used any time during the year, and adapted to different customer activities according to your market conditions and business needs.

You're better off concentrating on one or two of these ideas, planning and running them really well, rather than sponsoring a larger number of events for which you don't have the time or resources to get properly organised.

1. Planning tips

Once you've chosen the subject and dates for your special events, sit down and write a full plan for your attempts at media coverage and other local publicity efforts. Use the publicity checklists in Chapter 4 to prepare material suitable for editorial use.

Make up a complete timetable for your efforts, including the time you'll need to produce printed materials, press releases, media kits, advertising and promotional materials, coupons or giveaway items, as well as your stock schedule if you need to order special items for your event.

Look also for opportunities to enlist the aid of manufacturers in materials, people, films, literature, expertise, or any area where they could help you and tie into your event appropriately. You might be able to use coop materials or money (see Chapter 7).

You may be able to solicit merchandise prizes for contests, awards or draws. Show manufacturers how your event will benefit them in extra sales and publicity within your area. Make a list of products you'd be featuring in your event, and approach the manufacturers' salespeople with your idea.

2. Product promotion tips

A promotion involves careful product planning and stock control (or time control for service businesses), almost on a day-to-day level. Here are six guides to keep in mind.

1. When you are clearing old stock in a short-term 'loss leader' promotion, be careful to protect yourself by stating in all your advertising that only limited quantities are available.
2. If you use the 'list' or 'retail' price in the shop or in your ads, make sure you've really sold the featured items at that stated price over sufficient time to protect yourself against prosecution under the Trade Descriptions Acts.
3. If you run a competition, have your lawyer check it for complete legality.
4. If you are promoting new or current merchandise, make sure each department is stocked well enough to meet the full range of customer needs.
5. Check your departments to make sure that they are easy for staff to stock and maintain with a minimum of time and effort. (The time you save here could be put into selling.)
6. Above all, make sure that departments are easy to find and use, especially if your shop is primarily self-service.

3. Service promotion tips

Here are six guides to keep in mind when you're planning to promote your services:

1. Promote the items customers need most. Look for market needs your services can fill. You might be a first rate abstract painter or an expert in medieval music, but unless someone in your market place needs that service, it isn't saleable.
2. Concentrate on your strongest marketable skills. If you are, for example, a top-flight designer and an adequate writer, sell your artistic skills first. You can always hire someone else to do the things you don't do well.

3. If possible, have samples of your work or testimonials about your services from satisfied customers. People like to see what you could do for them and know who you've worked for, if possible. If you don't have samples, make them up to show what you could do; show off your talents.

4. Make it easy for customers to get in touch with you. Have a business card with your phone number on it, and invest in an answering machine or service to cover your phone when you're out selling.

5. Never miss a customer's deadline. If you agree to do something by 1 May, that doesn't mean 2 May. You've made an agreement, a deal, and you can't afford not to keep it. Fast, reliable, on-time service is *promotable*. Word gets out fast when you're not reliable.

6. Above all keep your current customers happy and informed. If you don't follow up and maintain good relationships, you won't have a base on which to build repeat business.

4. Checklist for organising promotions
As with any other business effort, the real secrets of successful sales promotion are in your appeal to your prospects and in staying well-organised so that you can meet prospects' expectations.

You should already know who your prospects are and what benefits will appeal to them. You have put yourself in the prospects' shoes enough to know what they need or want, where they are, and how best to reach them. The organising part is the administrative end that allows you to keep your promises to prospects and deliver the goods when you said you would.

The following checklist will assist you in organising a promotion that works for your business. Sections 2 to 5 can be used by any type of business; section 1 is for those involved in product sales only. Use the checklist any time you are planning a sales promotion effort.

A marketing manager of a major retail chain shared this list with us years ago, and encouraged us to share it with our readers. We have used this list ourselves as a basic guideline for helping retail clients stay organised.

PROMOTION PLANNING CHECKLIST

1. Merchandise availability

   (a) Will sufficient quantities be available in advance of promotion?
       - All products
       - All sizes
       - In required pack units
   (b) Will any new or seasonal merchandise be included?
       - New product line
       - New types
       - New sizes
       - New private label
   (c) Have suppliers been advised of planned increases in sales?
   (d) Have all deliveries been organised by times needed?

2. Proposition or offer

   (a) Is your 'total package' sufficiently competitive? Consider:
       - Pricing (Are price-lists complete, up to date?)
       - Discounts
       - Terms (special dating etc)
   (b) Is proposition going to be profitable?
       - Will the profit on merchandise promoted cover cost of programme, and still yield a worthwhile return?
       - Can you set up new accounts?
       - Can you displace competition in some places, customers or areas?
       - Can you add to profit through repeat orders?
   (c) Does programme provide any special motivation that may be needed to stimulate the expected selling and buying actions?
       - Special selling action by staff
       - Buying action by consumers
   (d) Are each of the above actions clearly understood and identified?

3. Timing

   (a) Do planned dates for programme conflict with other activities?
       - Other promotional programmes
       - Other activities of staff
       - Staff holidays
       - Other holidays
   (b) Does period of programme benefit from normal buying trend?
   (c) Consider competitive programmes (better be early — not later than competition).

4. Sales aids — sales training

   (a) Do staff sufficiently understand special merchandise offers?
       - Benefits to customer
       - Product knowledge
       - Special pricing
   (b) Merchandise demonstration
       - Samples needed?
       - Other supporting material?
   (c) Sales conferences or meetings planned for store staff?
       - Meeting outline available?
       - Visual aids — slides, films etc?
       - Other training materials needed?
   (d) Sales meetings planned with suppliers?
       - Meeting outline available?
       - Visual aids — slides, films etc?
       - Other training materials needed?

5. Communications and advertising

   (a) Have all communications/advertising objectives been identified?
       - Create awareness of your business or shop.
       - Provide sales leads.
       - Present and explain programme to staff, suppliers.
       - Develop interest, desire and action.
   (b) Has sufficient lead time been provided to execute communications/advertising plan?
       - Identify each separate element — mailing, sales aids, leaflets, newspaper, radio, TV, outdoor, other presentation and meeting materials. Distribution required and quantities spelled out.
       - Estimate production time for every item.
       - Add sufficient time for development, copy writing, design, review, revisions etc.
   (c) Has responsibility been clearly assigned for preparation of all items?
   (d) Is a control system in operation for assuring that the production timetable will be met, at every stage of preparation?
   (e) Have costs been estimated for all items, including artwork and production, postage etc? Are costs within budget?
   (f) Do you still have the enthusiasm you had when you started out with this great 'set-the-world-on-fire' idea?

Ideas for sales promotions

Listed below are ideas for events you can organise or sponsor and ideas for additional business-building promotions.

To work most effectively, the ideas you select should be adapted to your own shop or business image, as well as the resources you can muster.

These suggestions are simply to stimulate your own imagination — you may be able to come up with even more appropriate ideas. Some of them may seem similar to the community service ideas in Chapter 4, but these are more directly related to getting sales.

Your key to success is you! Some of these ideas will take more time, money, energy and planning than others. In all cases, the key to the success of your efforts to get customers involved will be in the careful attention and imagination you bring to them.

Though most of the detailed work in executing your plans can be delegated to reliable employees, it will be up to you to provide the guidance and vision that will help them help you make your plan a success.

1. Get families involved
Organise a Family Week with emphasis on activities that families can do together: camping, tennis, fishing, boating, golf, swimming, climbing — whatever is popular in your area.

You could have outdoor family refreshments for customers, show films, even organise a picnic for customer families at the end of your week with games and competitions for the youngsters and suitable small prizes for each.

2. Involve them in local history
Tie into any important local historical event. Ask your local history society for posters, old advertising material, antique clothes or equipment you could display, old photos, etc. Back your displays with Old-Fashioned Value Days with selected discounts and small prizes on your theme for customers.

3. Get them to come to a show — and become friends
Get together with five to ten other non-competitive retailers to hold a show in a local hall for a few days. Try to find complementary businesses and services.

If for example, you were in sporting goods, you might select speciality shops featuring casual wear, outdoor and indoor cooking utensils, toys and games, party and picnic supplies, mobile caravans, trailers or boats, your local travel agent, a local bank featuring financing for holidays and more expensive sports and leisure pastimes, and gift shops featuring sportsmen's gifts as some of your better prospects for this type of cooperation.

Organise fashion shows, demonstrations and customer events such as draws and contests tied into the show.

Tie all the advertising and displays into a central theme that is timely and promises a customer benefit as well (eg, 'Have more fun this summer' show).

Your rental, advertising, publicity and overhead costs can be split among participants on a cooperative basis, as well as merchandise prizes donated.

4. Get them to enjoy themselves

Organise a raffle, dance, sponsored walk or sports event to benefit a local charity.

5. Get them to draw or do crafts for you

Create an Arts Show that ties into your products or services with displays of drawings, photos and craft items submitted by local artists. Invite a committee of local people, including local counsellors and known patrons in business, to be the judges.

Award prizes in as many categories as you can dream up. Your most profitable prizes would be discount certificates toward the purchase of goods in your shop or business, but you can also award certificates or plaques for extra recognition value.

6. Get their children involved

Sponsor a poster contest in your local primary schools, generating interest through the teachers. Entries must be delivered personally at your business or shop by the child and one parent, and have one of your special entry forms attached (which gives you the family names and addresses for future mailings).

Categories should be organised by age for fair competition and chosen by a panel of teachers or other suitable judges.

Ask the editor of your local newspaper to reproduce the three or four best entries in the paper.

7. Get their teenagers involved
Feature local teenagers in a parade tied in with a community event. These can be outstanding young athletes or students chosen in a contest by their respective schools. They could ride on open-top buses or floats dressed by their clubs, with promoters' names prominently displayed.

8. Use popular local sports to get customers involved
Pick a popular local sport and build an intensive promotional week around it, including demonstrations, films, booklets or literature, special in-store and window displays, honouring outstanding local participants of that sport, a contest or other activities tied in to that sport, and selected loss leader or discount items as well.

9. Celebrate with your ethnic customers
If you have strong local ethnic groups, find out and celebrate their special holidays in your shop or business. Hold a party, invite civic leaders from that group, and celebrate their outstanding triumphs and figures in history.

10. Get customers to cook with you
Hold a barbecue cooking contest in your car park or local open space. Have entrants write down their recipes on the back of their entry forms in advance, so you can prepare a recipe collection for both entrants and other interested customers.

Your newspaper's women's editor may be interested in the recipes also. Present the idea with a good feature angle and time the press release to coincide with your contest.

You can have lots of fun with this contest. Promote male-female rivalry. Give disposable funny chef's hats and aprons to cookery contestants. Select a panel composed of both customers and local food authorities to judge the first prize winner and three runners-up.

You might even be able to organise local radio or television coverage for the event; check with the news or programming directors of your local stations, and send them advance material on it.

11. Let customers get to know your business letter
Create an Information Festival in cooperation with your local book shop and public library. (You may even get some of their

display space for your merchandise in return for displaying books and posters for them.)

Showcase books, demonstrations, new literature and films. You can cap it with a film festival of rented video films that tie in with the topics you want to feature. Involve local special interest groups in this.

12. Get customers to tell stories for you
Have a Tall Stories Contest for local fishermen, golfers, actors etc with prizes and audience judging on a special story-telling day. Get local dignitaries to participate and generate interest with leaflets, word of mouth, and advertising.

13. Get sports teams involved
Invite all your local college or secondary school sports teams to a special Open House celebrating Team Sports Day, with refreshments, spot prizes, a contest or draw, special discounts on your products or services.

14. Get customers competing
If fishing or archery is popular in your area, sponsor a Young Angler Contest (or Young Archer Contest) for girls and boys under 16 with parental approval.

Contestants must register and pick up their entry forms and rules at your shop or business with one parent. Parents must also be involved in certifying and photographing the youngster's catch, in the case of fishing. (Archery can be handled as a straight competition at the local butts with qualified judges etc.)

15. Get women who give parties involved
Hold a special series of selling parties for women. Feature recipes and entertainment tips for everything from picnics to buffets and formal dinners.

Get a local home economics teacher to give the demonstrations and compile recipes in a service booklet for your women customers.

You might also get cooperation from a local ladies' wear retailer to show home fashions.

16. Open your own seasons
Celebrate (or create) the opening day of any popular sports season or family activity (such as barbecues or picnics).

17. Celebrate your anniversary
Have a shop anniversary party with special gifts and door prizes.

18. Create a safety week
Create a special week with safety demonstrations, poster contests, displays featuring safety equipment etc. Try and involve your local health and safety officer, rescue services and the police.

19. Celebrate international holidays
October 10 is Health and Sports Day in Japan, which is celebrated as a national holiday. Get posters and display materials from a travel agent or tourist office. Offer some exotic prize — or even a dinner for two at your local Far Eastern restaurant. Find other ethnic and international events that could tie into your own business.

20. Offer group discounts
Promote a special discount card to civic clubs, service groups, or any of the groups you listed as appropriate sources of new business in your Chapter 2 worksheets.

Work out a discount offer that you can afford to keep effective for three months, then record all card sales on special forms. You'll probably be surprised at how much extra business a simple offer like this can bring you.

21. Send out calendars with your planned event
  dates on them
If you have planned all your major promotional events for the year, have them printed on handy wall or desk calendars with big spaces. Customers can do their own scheduling on your calendars and be reminded of your business's special events each month.

22. Offer customers prizes for new ways to use your
  product/service
This is another good technique to get customer involvement. Offer prizes of your own products or services, or other prizes with known general appeal. If you find customers coming up with enough good ideas, you may have a basis for approaching new customer groups, or selling more into your known markets.

Customers may be using your products and services already in ways that never occurred to you. Give them a chance to share new applications and ideas with you. You could even use the best ideas in your advertising.

23. *Make up sample packs for home or office use*
Even if your own product or service does not lend itself to this technique, you could find related but non-competitive, useful products that could serve as promotional gifts. You could use funny items as well.

Hire students or friends to deliver packages door to door or office to office in areas where you are likely to attract customers.

Your people should then get answers to a short shopping patterns type of questionnaire related to your own product or service. Also have them get prospect names and addresses, so you can follow up to see if prospects used and benefited from your gift. Give your people proper pre-qualifying questions, so they aren't just handing out samples indiscriminately. You want those gifts delivered only to people who could use your product or service.

24. *Have an auction*
Get together with non-competitive local businesses, and auction off your respective goods and services. If you have cash bidding and offer to donate a portion of the proceeds to a popular local charity, it might make your auction newsworthy. Or you could have customers or clients accumulate play money from your businesses during the promotional period, with which they would bid for the prizes.

25. *Offer customers a photo with purchase*
One building supply retailer organised a deal with a local photographer to take snapshots of customers or their families with every purchase over £10 in his store. He encouraged customers to bring their families, especially babies, into the store for the picture. Once both parents were in the store, he could show them his lines of childproof wallpaper, vinyl floor-coverings, and other building supplies of particular interest to young families.

26. *Sponsor a greeting card or cartoon contest for children*
Choose a topic of some general interest, related if possible to what your business does or sells. Tie the card idea into

Valentine's Day, Mother's Day, Father's Day, Christmas, or any other holiday. Offer to have 50 of the winner's cards printed up for the customer's own family to use.

Display all the runner-up cards in your premises or some other high-traffic spot in the community.

Cards must be handed in at your premises by the child and a parent, who signs the entry form giving you the name, address and phone number for you to follow up later.

27. Send your ad reprints to prospects
This is a simple way to get double use out of your advertising artwork, especially for industrial products or services. A simple reply card can be enclosed with your reprint, with a special offer or discount or information offer designed to generate enquiries.

28. Send out fake money towards the purchase of your products/service
Some pizza parlours and take-away restaurants already use this promotional technique to generate orders. You can make up play money or vouchers with slogans related to your business. Send it out with your catalogues, ad reprints or a special offer leaflet. Encourage customers to bring their money in to you for either a free gift, a demonstration, a discount on purchase, or some other benefit.

29. Reproduce old newspaper or magazine material with your business name or sales message on it
Take advantage of the trend to nostalgia, and find interesting material from old newspapers, magazines, advertisements or even posters.

Choose colourful material that the customer or prospect could frame and enjoy at home or in the office. Make sure your sales message is on the material somewhere, though not necessarily on the front. You'll be remembered.

30. Sponsor a local variety show or play
If you know of a church, school, social club or theatre group doing a show, sponsor them. You can exchange goods or services with them for a mention in their advertising, or advertise in their programmes.

Perhaps you could even get a sign put up for your business in the foyer on performance nights. If you are using tee shirts or other giveaways, give them to cast members so they can spread the word about your generosity — and your business. Get referral names from cast and backstage crew, too.

31. Have a spotter contest
If your product is easily identifiable in use, promote a contest where customers spotted using your product get a gift. Radio and television stations have been using this type of promotion spotting tee shirts, car stickers, and other giveaways featuring the station's identification or logo. Service businesses can use tee shirts, carrier bags and other giveaways too. For any business, this kind of walking promotion can provide extra free advertising.

32. Sponsor a beautiful baby contest in your area
Old-fashioned? Maybe. Effective? Definitely. Your customers and prospects are just as proud of their babies as anyone else. Award lots of prizes in as many different categories as you can, for example, prettiest picture of a baby with an animal, nicest smile, baby with the most personality etc.

Tie contest entries into purchase levels. With every £x purchase, the customer can enter another baby picture.

33. Try a continuing teaser mailing
Send out something with numerous component parts to prospects, one part at a time. Relate your sales message to each part, then have a salesperson deliver the final component personally.

One plant nursery owner sent a kitchen herb garden, sending first the potting seedbed, then the soil, then different seed packets with appropriate messages enclosed with each one. The salesperson then delivered the greenhouse top unit, which helped to propagate the herbs, with the intention of selling a garden tool and seed package. The mailing aroused real curiosity, and it worked as a selling introduction.

34. Send newsletters or service bulletins to prime prospects
You can use monthly or quarterly bulletins to inform prospects and customers of new trends affecting their lives or their industries.

Get a press cutting service, or have a staff member save appropriate items from available business reading. Rewrite the material into short, punchy, informative paragraphs. Helpful information on how to do business more profitably, or live better in any way is always welcome.

35. Give away tee shirts, carrier bags, or anything that could become a walking ad with purchases

If you have a catchy slogan, a memorable logo, or other attention-getting devices, put them on items to be given away according to various purchase levels.

The more people you have walking around with your advertising, the more awareness your giveaways can build for you.

36. Get your message airborne

You don't have to use a skywriter or message trailer behind a plane (though these can work well too) to get your message into the air. Give away balloons with your message on them.

Put your message on helium balloons and let them loose. Print your slogan on kites, and fly them. Have a kite-flying contest.

37. Make your business letters promotional tools

Make sure every letter from you is warm, clear, sympathetic, well-organised and complete. Your letters reflect you, and should assist the recipient in some way. Make your letter promote you.

38. Hold a seminar or demonstration on your premises

See the next section for how to do this successfully.

How to use a demonstration or seminar for promotion

The suggestions given below can be applied equally to seminars or demonstrations relating to product or service use, installation or 'how to do it' tips for customers.

What you decide to do will depend on the local availability of experts, resources or manufacturers to help you out, which topics would attract the most people in your own customer market, the size of your facilities, and which products or services you most wish to promote. Use the worksheet on page 107 to begin your planning.

You can also use these guidelines to ensure a successful open house or anniversary celebration.

1. Set practical objectives

Plan your demonstration from start to finish in advance, and set your objectives in terms of number of customers you wish to attract, projected costs, and what types of information you want your demonstration to convey.

Will you feature one product or service line or many? Will your demonstrator concentrate on educating, or selling, or both? Will the demonstrator be a staff member, a noted local person, or a manufacturer's salesperson?

2. Plan your timing

When is the best time of the day, week, month, and year to demonstrate this product line, or convey this information? Will you attract more people just before or just after the beginning of the local season for the products and/or services you're featuring? What kind of advertising and promotional messages for this event would best attract *your* customers?

3. Plan media coverage

Analyse the local media and market to decide which will prove the most effective way to get customers into the shop for your event. How much newspaper, radio, TV or direct mail coverage will you need to reach the majority of your prospects?

Which are the best media to reach the specific customer groups you want within your trade area? (For example, if you want to reach young families, is there one newspaper, magazine or radio station that would reach this group more cost effectively than others?)

4. Try personal invitations

Would personal letters or invitations to known or preferred customers prove cost-efficient and effective, and build more goodwill?

5. Check for editorial and news opportunities

Analyse your opportunities for getting good editorial coverage of the event beforehand in your local media: is there enough news or feature value in your event to convince an editor that it would be useful for readers to know about?

If your invited demonstrator is particularly noteworthy, your topic is of public interest, or you're doing something that's never been done in your area, chances are you can interest at least one editor. Can you spot any related public relations opportunities inherent in your event?

6. Check your equipment needs
Check with the demonstrator, and go over which of the following equipment he or she might need: audio-visual aids, projector and screen, special lights, chalkboard or easels, a low table for demonstrations, a lectern for notes, sound equipment.

7. Plan where your supplies will go
Also make up a complete list of products, brochures about your services, and supplies from the shop or office that must be on hand. Decide beforehand where each will be placed in the demonstration area for convenient handling, in the sequence needed.

8. Plan your space requirements
How much space will be needed, and where, for the number of customers you anticipate? Analyse your shop or office layout to decide which space could best be cleared for seating and how you need to temporarily reorganise furniture or floor stock and displays.

9. Plan for displays
Make sure your plans include having displays appropriate to the subject matter of the event right next to where your customers will be, so there will be visual reminders of the products or services being sold.

10. Organise all elements
How many chairs will you need, and where will they come from? Will you need a stage, a platform, or other special effects? Add these to your master list of things to be organised.

11. Make customers comfortable
Organise extra touches for customer comfort: free, fresh coffee and tea, ashtrays, a waste bin, notepads and pencils (with your name on them, of course), a supervised play area for the smaller children (featured in all advertising and promotional material as an extra draw for younger parent groups), spot prizes or draws.

12. Let people know where you are
Both before, and on the day of your event, plan for plenty of in-store, window, and outside directional signs. Also place signs prominently in and around the demonstration areas on the big day.

13. Rehearse the demonstration with your experts

Make sure the demonstrator is fully rehearsed and knowledgeable. Go over the presentation for product or service knowledge and demonstration techniques until you're satisfied that it will flow smoothly, and that the demonstrator can answer questions well.

If necessary, go through a role-playing session where you ask all the questions you can think of, no matter how silly they seem. Customers will be there because they don't know something and want to.

14. Be sure everything will be clear to customers

Make sure the demonstrator can explain points clearly so that even the most ignorant customer could understand them.

Be alert to the speaker's use of jargon or technical terms that could confuse your customers. If necessary, be prepared to produce a glossary sheet of terms and phrases that the customer could take home.

15. Last-minute extras to check

On the big day, make sure all supplies and materials are in the right place, as previously discussed, and well organised for easiest demonstration.

Detail a staff member to make sure extra chairs are brought in as needed. Have extra ashtrays, chairs, literature, giveaways, or other supplies on hand where they can be reached easily.

Check that signs are clear, readable, and logically placed for maximum exposure. Test all tools and equipment, audio-visual aids, and anything else that could go wrong.

16. Provide for customer follow-up

Get as many names and addresses of attenders as possible, either through a door prize, a raffle, a competition entry, a visitors' book, or personal solicitation of names and addresses by your staff.

Send them a follow-up letter with a check sheet they can use to evaluate and give you feedback on your event. (Make sure you include a prepaid reply envelope or stamp to make it as easy as possible for them to reply.)

17. Find out about customer likes and dislikes

Find out as much as you can, in as brief and easy-to-answer a form as possible, about how your customers feel both about the particular demonstration and your business in general. This will help you in setting up future demonstrations and in evaluating each one.

18. Evaluate your demonstration

Your assessment of the demonstration's success will depend on your original objectives for the demonstration. If it was purely educational, your head count and audience reactions will be your guide.

Revenue, both on the demonstrated products and related items sold that day, will guide you to an evaluation of a selling demonstration.

19. Analyse business increases

Analyse the traffic or business increases on the day of the event and the following week or two. Compare pre-demonstration with post-demonstration sales and amounts per sale, not only in the featured department or service but overall.

See if you can detect any spin-off value in general interest that your demonstration could have generated.

20. Make your demonstration work for customers

The primary point to remember throughout is to create your demonstration, seminar, open house or special event from the customer's point of view.

Present the benefits, the 'what's in it for me to go there?' to your customers in all your advertising and promotional materials.

If you have a clear idea of your customers' real needs, you're much more likely to put on a successful and profitable demonstration or event that will also build goodwill and better community relations for your shop.

How to use displays to build sales

Here are some of the secrets that top retailers use to make in-store displays more attractive and 'selling'. Even in an office where you are selling personal services, you can adapt some of these 10 retail-oriented tips to show customers what you're selling.

1. Make displays visible

If you're featuring a general item or idea, place your display where all your customers can see it — preferably near the main door and checkout counter.

2. Put related items together
Keep specific range or product displays as near as possible to the merchandise being featured.

3. Make merchandise accessible
Wherever you can, make it possible for customers to touch or hold your merchandise so they can examine it more fully. Even if you have to bolt or chain some products down, make sure they're able to be seen as clearly as possible.

4. Keep signs and materials readable
Make sure all your displays are clear and readable and positioned where customers can see or read them easily.

5. Hang mobile displays carefully
If you're hanging a unit or display from the ceiling, make sure it's hung low enough to be looked over easily, but not low enough to get tangled up with customers or staff.

6. Don't hide stock under displays
Don't conceal merchandise with your displays unless you're storing extra stock. In that case, make sure it's still easy for staff to bring out stock from behind or under your display.

7. Choose display locations wisely
Never put your displays where your staff will have to move them in order to deal with your customers.

8. Light displays well
Always place your displays in a well-lighted position.

9. Use all available space
Use your windows, pavements or even part of your parking area for eye-catching displays whenever you can, especially when you're tying them into a promotion for the whole store.

10. Display customer services too
Wherever you can, use counter cards, wall posters or other display aids to point out customer services (eg, credit plans, credit cards accepted, delivery terms, or new products).

WORKSHEET FOR DEMONSTRATION OR SEMINAR IDEAS

1. Which of my products or services lend themselves to a demonstration or seminar? Which benefits or applications could be shown well?

   Product or service: Benefit or application to
                                       be shown:

   _____   _____

   _____   _____

2. Which prospect/customer groups would be most interested, and why?

   Prospect/customer group: Why they would be interested:

   _____   _____

   _____   _____

3. How many people can I fit into my location?_____
   Is there another location that would work better?_____

4. Who would do the demonstration?_____

5. What materials, supplies and visual aids would I need?_____

   _____

6. How could I most effectively reach prospect groups to invite them to my demonstration and get their commitment (eg, telephone, ads etc)?

   _____

   _____

What is direct mail?

Direct mail is direct response advertising. Direct response advertising is a sales message sent through the mail or appearing in the media that asks the prospect to *do* something: to cut out and return a coupon, to buy your product or service, to ask for more information, or to come into your business for a deal or a demonstration.

The most important ingredient here is the *call to action*. Direct response advertising is always *measurable*, because you have included a coupon, order form, certificate or other mechanism that *allows you to count* the number of people who bring it in. You have a physical record of the effectiveness of your campaign.

Since a prospect has to bring in or post your coupon to get the benefit, you can tell within days whether your advertising is actually building sales for you. You can also find out your average sales per order, profit per order, and whether or not you were able to sell related products or services to respondents.

Many of the ideas listed earlier in this chapter involve the use of response mechanisms, particularly to get customer and prospect names and addresses. When you are selecting or creating your own sales promotion ideas, whether special events, demonstrations, or special-offer sales, look for ways to include response mechanisms that will tell you more about your customers and prospects.

A direct mail piece should follow the guidelines for advertising listed in Chapter 6.

1. Using coupons, contests and draws to get customer names

Coupon promotions and their variations, which include gift vouchers, contests, lotteries and draws, provide one of the fastest, most inexpensive ways to get potential customers into your shop or warehouse, so you can find out more about them.

A coupon promotion involves using a printed coupon to offer customers a free gift, a discount on selected items that you know are of general interest in your market, or a discount based on a percentage off purchases.

In order to cash in the coupon, the customer has to post it to you or come to your location. Also (and this is *most* important), the customer has to give you his or her name, address and phone number on the coupon to get the benefit.

This is critical for two reasons: first, you need to know where customers live or work so you can eventually pinpoint them when you're analysing your customer mix; second, you need their addresses and phone numbers for your follow-up research, as well as your future mailing list.

In effect, you are using your coupon advertising to do a preliminary test for your market. Whether you decide to use a direct mail campaign to surrounding neighbourhoods, leaflets passed out on the street, or a newspaper ad, the point is to bring potential customers into your location or get them to respond to and buy the products or services you sell.

Coupons can also be used to generate customer leads for your sales people to follow up. That means your advertising has to: give the customer a good reason to buy; ask for the order; encourage the customer to come to you; and make the time limit and conditions for redemption of the coupon perfectly clear.

Coupon testing is a way to find out how well your idea will work — whether you can get customers to buy from you (preferably on a regular basis).

You can also do a test to find out whether newspaper, leaflets, or direct mail works best when you're trying to build business, and which products or services you offer bring in the most customers.

2. Other ways to get names

There are a number of other ways to get people to give you their names and addresses. One is to hold a contest or draw. Check with the local authority for legal procedures and regulations.

Choose a first prize of significant value and general appeal that ties into your business, or uses products you sell. For example, you could offer £100-worth of time, services or products of the customer's choice. Then choose a number of less expensive prizes of graduated value, so more people will feel they have a chance to win.

Fix a six-week time limit on the contest, starting at the time your advertising reaches your prospects.

Another way to get names — and business — is to use gift vouchers. The gift voucher buyers fill out a simple request and order form with the names and addresses of both giver and receiver on it. They bring the order form into your shop to get the voucher itself. You get two opportunities for business, one of which is guaranteed.

Also, you can always offer buyers of gift vouchers a bonus gift or selected discount in your original advertising, as an incentive to come in.

3. Keep complete records

To know whether your test is working, and how well, you need complete and accurate records of every step you take in your campaign. You need to know what types of direct mail you sent or gave out, who it went to, and how much each element cost you.

You also need records of what you sold from each ad and what extra sales your staff were able to build on to your original offer.

It's easier than it sounds. Because your customers have had to present a coupon, order form or voucher, it's a simple step to make sure your staff record the actual amount of sale at the time of redemption.

When you're having the piece designed, leave a box or blank space for your eventual office sales record. Then it takes only a moment at the time of sale to write in the sale amount, items sold or whatever other information you decide you need.

You'll have to make sure the recording is done on every sale.

Once you have itemised daily and weekly records, complete with customer names and addresses, you're ready to do some preliminary analysing.

First, compare your sales and gross margins with your cost records for the whole period of your test.

Find out exactly where you stand. Did you break even, lose money or make money overall? Keep in mind that since it's a test you can't expect miracles. If you did break even or make money, consider yourself fortunate. It's a nice side benefit that enhances the real purpose of the test, which is to get enough names of potential customers to find out whether you have a profitable market.

On the next page you will find a six-week result chart that you can use for your own contests, coupon promotions or direct mail. Record all the factors shown in terms of your own efforts.

Measuring the results of all promotions

If you tie your sales promotion ideas into purchase levels or service sales, you will have an exact measure of the extra revenue generated by your promotional activity.

Compare your sales volume during the promotion to your previous year's volume (if you have been established for more than a year). Break down all your costs, including a proportion of your regular administration and overheads, based on the time and materials involved in doing your promotion.

Once you have done this, you will know the amount of your sales return compared with your promotional investment. There is no ideal return percentage, as each business and promotion will involve different cost and sales factors. You will need to judge for yourself whether the tangible sales returns and intangible returns in consumer awareness justify your time and cost investment in the promotion.

SIX-WEEK REPORT ON MAILING PIECE RESULTS 198X

Fill in functions by these key numbers where possible:

1. Get orders for _____.
2. Get orders for _____.
3. Enquiries/leads only.
4. Get cash/credit orders.
5. Give information.
6. Get information.
7. Build lists.
8. Other (fill in below).

Fill in the dates and number of replies received for each week. Where cash value comes in, give round figures for money or orders received.

Data on mailing piece	Week 1	2	3	4	5	6
1. Function: _____ Date posted: _____ No. sent: _____ Response: ☐ Excellent ☐ Fair ☐ Good ☐ Poor ☐ Disaster	Dates: Replies (no)	Replies (no)	Replies (no)	Replies (no)	(Replies no)	Replies (no)
2. Function: _____ Date posted: _____ No. sent: _____ Response: ☐ Excellent ☐ Fair ☐ Good ☐ Poor ☐ Disaster	Dates: Replies (no)	Replies (no)	Replies (no)	Replies (no)	(Replies no)	Replies (no)

111

3. Function: _____
   Date posted: _____
   No. sent: _____
   Response:
   ☐ Excellent ☐ Fair
   ☐ Good ☐ Poor ☐ Disaster

   Dates:
   Replies (no) | Replies (no) | Replies (no) | Replies (no) | (Replies no) | Replies (no)

4. Function: _____
   Date posted: _____
   No. sent: _____
   Response:
   ☐ Excellent ☐ Fair
   ☐ Good ☐ Poor ☐ Disaster

   Dates:
   Replies (no) | Replies (no) | Replies (no) | Replies (no) | (Replies no) | Replies (no)

5. Function: _____
   Date posted: _____
   No. sent: _____
   Response:
   ☐ Excellent ☐ Fair
   ☐ Good ☐ Poor ☐ Disaster

   Dates:
   Replies (no) | Replies (no) | Replies (no) | Replies (no) | (Replies no) | Replies (no)

6. Function: _____
   Date posted: _____
   No. sent: _____
   Response:
   ☐ Excellent ☐ Fair
   ☐ Good ☐ Poor ☐ Disaster

   Dates:
   Replies (no) | Replies (no) | Replies (no) | Replies (no) | (Replies no) | Replies (no)

Chapter 6
Using Advertising Effectively

Choosing and scheduling your media cost — effectively

Here's how to make sure that you reach and motivate the people you want to sell to — and that your advertising money will go where it will give you the greatest benefit.

1. Define your objectives
Your first step is to write down and organise everything you want your advertising to accomplish for your business within the year: the markets you want to reach and the sales volume you want to generate.

You may have three or four basic objectives that you want your advertising to help you meet.

2. Write them down
Whatever you decide, write down both major and minor objectives, with dates, numbers, or percentages precisely spelled out. This gives you a basic set of goals and an idea of your timing. The next steps are who and how.

3. Who's your market?
Each objective requires that you have someone to sell to. Your first step is to pinpoint your audience by categories in their order of importance to your selling effort. Who are your most important customer groups?

Your audiences will vary in their make-up and in their importance to you according to the population, your geographic area and the mix of people or businesses you wish to serve.

Your own sales and delivery records, credit records, or other active customer records can help you pinpoint who your customers are, what they buy, and where they're located. If you have already done some direct response advertising, you should already have a valuable record and picture of your market to help you sell more effectively to them.

4. Choose a mix of media that will reach most customers
Your next step is to choose the media and formats that will best help you reach your market specifically and consistently. Remember, each format has specific advantages and limitations. Be sure to choose a *balance* of media that will give you the fullest possible market coverage for the time and money you've allocated for your campaigns.

You may want to use newspapers to reach a large mass audience, backed up by selected direct mail, and radio campaigns for special sales.

No one medium will reach *all* of your market regularly. You need a good mix of media to ensure that your advertising is selling for you all the time, to as many prospects as possible.

Here's how the media mix can best be used to build traffic and sales for you:

(a) NEWSPAPERS
Newspapers are a top choice for a timely or newsworthy ad. This can include the announcement of a new product, a special sale or in-store demonstrations. Your newspaper ad should tie into a special sale, the opening of a new location, new services, or events such as holidays.

Put your ads where your customers will see them. Keep your prospects in mind when choosing where to place your ads; select a position on the sports or business pages if your target is men and on the family living or women's pages if it's women. Use the news or business sections for business-oriented advertising.

If you don't consider yourself creative or . do not have creative talent available, try a discount or special-offer coupon. These days, there are no better attention-getters for price-conscious consumers.

(b) MAGAZINES
Small business people and retailers have generally avoided advertising in national magazines because of the high cost. However, there are a number of regional and county magazines that offer valuable advertising opportunities for the local business. Local newspapers also publish occasional magazines that feature special topics such as leisure, motoring and home improvements.

They have been working to attract more new business from local small business, service and manufacturing business and from retailers and their suppliers. But before you select a regional edition or local magazine, be sure to find out how many of your potential customers read it. Ask the salesperson for circulation figures, and what groups of people those figures represent.

(c) RADIO

With radio, it's important to know the demographics (the make-up) of your target market. If your prospects are mostly men, you will probably want to place your commercials during sports broadcasts, near the news, and in or near other regular shows that have predominantly male audiences. Choose your station carefully, too. Concentrate on news and easy listening stations to reach business people driving home from work. For women at home, daytime is your prime time.

Here are a few script tips for using radio commercials to advantage. If you are composing your own commercial (or 'spot'), remember the time constrictions that radio poses. Your words alone must provide the punch. Choose words precisely and carefully. Write the message simply by repeating the points you want to convey, and steer clear of unnecessary details.

Most commercials run about two words per second, so a 30-second spot should be no longer than 60 words to fit the time. If you want sound effects, your radio salesperson can help you organise them.

(d) TELEVISION

There is no need to dismiss television as too costly any more. Though prime time may be too expensive, spot commercials aired late at night or during the day can be affordable.

Cable TV, soon to be available, will offer you an exciting and reasonably priced advertising alternative.

Check with your regional ITV station salesperson about how much production help and services you can get in preparing your scripts and visuals for television spots. Keep your visuals as simple and inexpensive as possible, and check the message for clarity and completeness. Channel Four offers a very reasonably priced package to first-time advertisers.

Make sure you run your spots adjacent to the programmes most likely to attract the viewers to whom you want your message delivered.

(e) YELLOW PAGES

Unlike the other media discussed, the Yellow Pages is unique in that it is actually a consumer's guide that prospects refer to once they've made up their minds to buy.

For businesses having difficulty coordinating advertising plans and monitoring their effectiveness, the Yellow Pages offers a unique opportunity to stretch your promotional budget.

Because your Yellow Pages ad will be listed among those of your competitors, promoting your special or unique services is essential. You can also use an attractive ad that will be eye-catching on the page.

(f) OTHER MEDIA

Direct mail is an ideal way to reach a group chosen on the basis of income, prior purchase or similar criterion, provided your mailing list is accurate and up to date, as covered in Chapter 2.

If you want to reach an entire trade or profession, consider an insertion in the trade/professional journal that is most widely read.

There has been a growth in recent years in free newspapers. They have now been accepted by readers and advertisers alike, and they offer a very effective advertising medium for local business.

Outdoor advertising in the form of posters, and bus and tube cards also keep your message in front of your prospects on a daily basis.

5. *Make a master plan*

Timing your efforts is the next important step. You need a full media plan and schedule to keep your production team on track and to make sure each season's objectives are filled. Refer back to Chapter 1 for your product timing considerations.

Sit down with a calendar and work out exactly when you want to advertise in each medium, week by week over an entire year. How many newspaper pages will you need? How many radio spots, direct mail shots, TV commercials or whatever — and when? Then write it down on a master plan.

Put every sale, promotion, contest or special offer, with its advertising requirements, into a yearly master plan. Make sure that this master plan is designed to fit the marketing and sales objectives you have set for your business.

Study your own business and the market place in which you operate. Familiarise yourself with the important media so you know which media mix will best reach *your* prospects. Then you'll be sure of getting full value from your budget.

Once you have your schedule lined up, you can plan your monthly cash flow for production, space costs, air time, mailing, buying supplies etc. That way you'll know when your major expenses are due. Plan your cash flow so you won't have to take out any loans, if possible.

Now, use the worksheet on page 119 to evaluate and organise your own media plan with costs and timing.

6. *Keep track of the response*

Don't forget that your staff are an important part of your team, and should help you keep your response records up to date.

If you already have staff filling and recording orders, all you need is to be certain that they log the orders from your promotion or advertising in such a way that you can keep track of them.

Orders from direct mail, newspaper, TV or radio advertising should be keyed and filed in such a way that you can extract them easily from your regular sales slips or delivery forms. This is so you can evaluate how well your advertising worked, and how much you sold from it. Wherever possible, include a reply coupon with your ad, and *always* with a direct mail shot. Ensure that you get *some* response. The prospect should be offered the chance to stay on your mailing list and you will have his other name and address, and may make a sale another time. The coupon should be coded to indicate its source.

For telephone orders, you can train your staff to ask the customer where he or she heard or saw your advertising or promotional material, so the source can be coded on to the order slip.

If you do a coupon or discount voucher campaign, you must have someone keep up your record of orders received daily.

In retail, your sales staff and records clerk should work in cooperation, to be sure that your stock of featured items is sufficient and that the total amount of the sale, including related items, is recorded on every coupon or voucher received.

Make up a special abbreviated record code for your staff to make it faster and, perhaps, tie it into an incentive plan, to be sure you get all the information you need for accurate evaluation.

You can use your present staff by retraining them to handle advertising responses. Or you can employ and train someone part time just to coordinate your record keeping.

MEDIA EVALUATION / COSTING WORKSHEET

1. In which local media should I be advertising to reach the majority of prospects in my three most important customer groups?

2. How often and when should I be advertising? (Review your product life cycle information in Chapter 1; determine the frequency of purchase.)

Daily, local and free newspapers

Name	Audience	Line rate	Ad size	Cost per ad

Estimated production costs:_____ Number of ads:_____
Production assistance available:_____
Date of first ad:_____ Deadline for material:_____

Sales representatives	Phone	Office located at

Total yearly projected cost for advertising in all chosen newspapers:

Radio stations

Name	Type of audience	Spot length	Cost per spot	No of spots

Estimated production costs:_____ Sound effects?:_____
Production assistance available:_____
Date of first commercial:_____ Deadline for material:_____
Script assistance available:_____
Total yearly projected cost for advertising in all chosen radio stations:

Television stations

Name	Type of audience	Spot length	Cost per spot	No of spots

Sales representatives	Phone	Office/studio located at

Estimated production costs:_____
Slides or visuals needed:_____
Production assistance available:_____
Script assistance available:_____
Date of first commercial:_____ Deadline for material:_____

MEDIA EVALUATION/COSTING WORKSHEET

Sales representatives   *Phone*   *Studio located at*

_____   _____   _____

Total yearly projected costs for advertising in all chosen TV stations:

_____

Other media that would reach my customers and prospects

Medium	*Target audience*	*Dates*	*Costs*
Poster sites	_____	_____	_____
Yellow Pages	_____	_____	_____
Suppliers' leaflets	_____	_____	_____
Catalogues	_____	_____	_____
Direct mail	_____	_____	_____
Local magazines	_____	_____	_____
Business or trade magazines			
_____	_____	_____	_____
_____	_____	_____	_____

Magazine production assistance available: _____

Estimated production costs:_____ Photos needed?_____

Magazine reps	*Phone*	*Deadlines*	*Address for materials*
_____	_____	_____	_____

Total yearly projected cost of advertising in chosen magazines:

_____

Medium	*Target audience*	*Dates*	*Costs*
Free papers	_____	_____	_____
Discount coupons	_____	_____	_____
Other:			
_____	_____	_____	_____

Total yearly project cost — all media: £

Space or time costs	_____
Production costs	_____
Creative fees	_____
Illustration costs	_____
Admin/other costs	_____
TOTAL COSTS	_____
My objective in increased sales revenue	_____
My projected return on advertising investment	_____ %

(Revenue divided by cost equals return percentage.)

Finding local advertising and promotion specialists

It takes special skills to put together a persuasive and attractive advertising campaign. Even if you *could* write, illustrate (or announce), assemble and produce your advertising single-handed, you wouldn't have time to run your business.

As a business owner, you don't have the skills or training to do an effective job by yourself. But you can get together a part-time staff of specialists to help you. In every community, no matter how small, you can find people who make their living providing the kinds of services you need.

Here's how you can find people in your community to help you prepare and produce an effective advertising or promotion campaign — without costing you a fortune.

1. Agency help

In larger towns and cities, you'll find that an advertising agency can help you plan, produce, and coordinate your entire campaign. A full-service agency has writers, artists, production people for all media, printers, typesetters, and photographers available to work on your account. You tell them what you need, your objectives, and your budget. They do the rest.

If you plan an extensive campaign, an agency that understands your market and your advertising needs can save you invaluable time and effort in preparing an effective advertising programme. You also have a ready source of creative, technical, and production expertise to draw on for specialised areas such as TV, radio, direct mail, magazine, and print advertising.

They solve your marketing and advertising production problems, leaving you free to concentrate on your business. But if you're in a small town, or can't use an advertising agency, what can you do then? Find out who else can help you in your area.

2. Look for these people

To help you create and prepare your advertising in print, you need a copywriter and layout artist familiar with advertising techniques. Your layout artist should also be able to do artwork if necessary, though many printers and typesetters offer this service.

(Artwork is the process of pasting up all the pictures and copy that go into your ad, so it's ready for printing. A layout is a plan, usually a drawing, of the way your ad will look when it's printed. The artist uses the layout as a guideline when producing the artwork of your ad for the printer, newspaper or magazine.)

These specialists are usually available on a freelance basis, when you buy their services at an hourly rate for the time they spend on your advertising. Generally, they're listed in your Yellow Pages under 'Artists — Commercial and Industrial', 'Designers — Advertising and Graphic', 'Publicity Consultants', 'Advertising Agencies' etc.

Get them to show you samples of work they have done for other businesses. You'll get an idea of how they work. Ask about results. Did their work create sales? How many?

You can often find these professionals through your local newspaper, your printer, or even by word of mouth. Most newspapers and magazines have special design and/or copy services that you, as an advertiser, can use. Simply ask them what they offer. They'll be happy to help you.

If you plan to use radio or TV advertising, your local radio or TV station can often be helpful. Call the advertising department. Often the salespeople themselves can help you. If you need a lot of help with production, they have specialists on the staff who can advise you and studios where you can have your commercials taped or filmed.

In major cities, you can find production or audio-visual houses that specialise in TV commercials. Go to the experts for your scriptwriting, direction and production.

3. Printing services

Your local area probably has at least one printer or typesetter who can help you with non-newspaper print advertising. Again, check the Yellow Pages.

Shop around for prices, quality and services. Find out how much they're able or willing to help you. If possible, have them give you an estimate of costs for doing an ad you really plan to use.

Look at work they have done, to check for quality and accuracy of typesetting and printing. If possible, find out how much other ads they have produced cost their customers.

Good printers and typesetters are usually cooperative, both in giving you an estimate on your planned ads and in showing you samples of work they have done for others. They can often act as consultants when you have a problem in production of your material.

4. A few tips to get better results

When you're looking for people or services, don't always choose the cheapest — unless they're also the best. Look for quality, ideas, service, and results as well as costs.

For direct response especially, you need methods that will bring in sales you can count. A direct response copywriter can usually tell you how well his or her ads worked — if not in exact numbers, with a close estimate. Part of his or her job is to find out how many responses the offer pulled on each ad or promotion. They can help you find out which offers work best, if they don't already know. A good copywriter should be able to act as a consultant, as well as a writer.

A designer should have a feel for what will draw readers into the page, the ad, or the brochure — and what will attract prospects to use a coupon or voucher.

Direct response is hard-sell advertising. You're asking the customer to act. Your graphics must move the customer through your message and into the order form. A good designer will know how.

Whoever you hire, make sure they know how to help you get *action* from your advertising. Have a clear picture of what action you want to get, so you can help them in every way possible. Give them all the market knowledge and advertising or promotion sales expertise you can. Then let them get on with their job. They're your experts. The results should be a coordinated, *motivating* campaign that will bring you *sales*.

CHECKLIST OF LOCAL SPECIALISTS

Name	Phone	Skill or service	Cost/fee

Advertising that stands out and sells

Even if you never write a word of your ads yourself, here are proven copy techniques for sales success that you should look for in every ad you produce.

These tips are based on our 15 years of experience in copywriting. Our copy has helped clients sell nearly a million pounds every year in goods and services, even in the tightest economic climates. You can profit by our experience, and by that of other professionals before us from whom we learned many of these valuable lessons.

1. Ads must sell

The first lesson of good direct marketing is that every ad you produce should *sell*. Not announce. Not brag. Just sell. Persuade. Convince. Ask for action, and bring in sales for you.

In your business, though not in all businesses, any ad that doesn't sell your goods, services, the convenience of ordering by mail from you, or whatever else you want to sell, is wasting your money.

It is not enough to say, 'We're having a spectacular summer sale' or 'Christmas bargains'. Though that may attract the customers who are already looking for what you have to offer, your ad should do much more than that.

You have to show even non-customers what you have to offer *them*, convince them of their need or desire for your product or service, give them reasons to buy, and get them to buy from *you*. That takes a combination of good selling techniques, copy that is full of benefits, and a basic knowledge on your part of *how people buy*, especially your own customers.

When you're advertising to customers or prospects, keep yourself in the background and talk to them. Use the 'you' voice in your copy. Don't say 'we have' when you can use 'you can get' or 'here's how you' or 'here's why you need' or any other you-oriented approach.

Don't sell products — sell customers on buying your products. Your customers aren't interested in your need to sell. They are only interested in what they're going to get if they buy from you.

When you're advertising, be scrupulously honest in all copy and service claims. Don't offer a sale with only a few items in stock. Even when you tell customers the quantity is limited, they're likely to be upset if they don't get their order. Don't offer a two-week delivery service if it's likely to take four.

When selling by mail order, you are legally bound to offer delivery within 28 days and must state the delivery time in your printed matter. Your address must appear in full in such mail order advertisements, as well as on the order form.

Above all, be sure that you don't over-claim the value of your product or service in your copy.

You can use all the emotional benefit-loaded descriptions you like, but if the product doesn't back them up, your customers won't buy from you again. (You may think that's fine, since you have their money, but you lose the opportunity of repeat or new product orders, which could be your best source of quick turnover.)

Your copy doesn't have to be dry or dull to be honest, but it must reflect the integrity of your operation and your product lines. Better to understate than to over-claim.

2. *Advertisement content*

You may have heard of the 'AIDA' formula for successful direct response selling in any medium:

(a) Attract Attention
(b) Build Interest
(c) Arouse Desire
(d) Then ask for Action

The trick is to pack as many benefits as possible into your headline and first paragraph of copy. Selling points can come in further down in the body copy.

Making sure all your copy offers benefits will help you hold and interest consumers, even those who weren't necessarily looking for your product.

When you do finally ask for action, show customers how to act. Give them a coupon to send in, or a freefone number to call, or both. As an extra incentive to act, offer them a gift or a chance to enter a contest or a premium for responding quickly.

Make sure that you offer both a benefit for acting and clear, specific ways in which to act. The easier you make it for the customer to order, the more orders you're likely to get. Design your coupons so that even the laziest customer can act.

The basic lesson here is that benefits *sell*. Even if you're putting clusters of products together in a single ad, copy and headlines that are loaded with benefits can help you get and keep the customer's attention all the way through the ad.

If you combine these copy tips with a clean, consistent layout and an appropriate range of products selected carefully for your markets, you can start building advertising campaigns that really bring in the orders.

The two checklists following will help you ensure that your ads will *sell* for you, both in your copy and your visual presentation. Use them to check ads that you are running now and ads you plan to run.

COPY AND LAYOUT CHECKLIST FOR PRINT ADVERTISING

☐ Is your headline directed to the reader and his or her interests?

☐ Do you promise the reader the benefits of buying at your shop, buying your products, or becoming a client for your services?

☐ Is the headline as brief as you can make it without missing the point?

☐ Does your entire ad emphasise one basic idea (eg, lower prices, better service, wider range of stock etc)?

☐ Do you present the product, service or store selling points that show the customers how their benefits will be delivered (eg, you get a more professional looking job etc)?

☐ Do you compliment the prospect where you can?

☐ Is all the copy clear and easy to read and understand?

☐ Do you use guarantees and other means to build customer confidence in your products, your services, or your store wherever possible?

☐ Does your copy give the reader good reasons and excuses for buying?

☐ Do you make it as easy as possible for the customer to order?

☐ Do you tell customers clearly how, when and where they can buy your advertised features?

☐ Does your advertising sell for *you alone*, or could it just as easily work for another business, service, product or shop?

☐ Does every ad *ask for the order*?

☐ Is your basic layout clean, clear and uncluttered?

☐ Are your illustrations large or detailed enough to show the products featured accurately?

☐ Do you show the product in action or the service being given (or in use) where possible?

☐ Is the layout attention-getting? Will it stand out in a newspaper filled with other advertising?

☐ Is the visual style of your ads consistent? Does it build a good visual image of your store or business?

☐ Do all the typestyles coordinate well on the page? Are your typefaces in the same basic family of types (except for special emphasis), or do you have a clutter of different styles on the same page?

☐ Does the layout lead the reader's eye all through the ad, or does it encourage skipping or, worse still, page turning? (Note that a reader's eyepath starts at the upper left corner and ends at the lower right corner, with numerous darts and jumps in between as various elements catch the reader's interest.)

☐ Are your lines of type short enough for comfortable reading? Is there enough space between the lines to look attractive and inviting?

☐ Is all your type large enough to read easily?

☐ If you use white copy reversed out of black, do you check it carefully for both readability and reproduceability?

☐ When you use a second colour, does it highlight the most important elements of your ad?

☐ Do you check carefully to see what the visual effect will be?

☐ Does your shop or business or product logo stand out consistently? (The logo is a visual symbol that stands for your business.)

☐ Is your shop or business or brand name easy to see and instantly identifiable?

☐ If you have maps in your ad, are they clear and easy to use?

☐ Most important, do you *plan* your layouts ahead of time instead of leaving them until the last minute and throwing them together? Plan a consistent campaign style that leaves you plenty of room to add new elements without destroying your ad's image and visual effectiveness.

Chapter 7

Coop Advertising Saves Money

What is coop advertising?

Cooperative advertising, also known as coop, is a process in which two or more parties share the costs of advertising or promotion. The two parties could be a manufacturer and a retailer (or salesperson), two retailers or two business owners. They are cooperating by pooling money to buy more advertising or promotional materials than one party could get alone. The term is American, though the practice is common enough in the UK.

One of the most common forms of coop advertising that you see regularly is the coupons that food and service manufacturers send to customers to offer discounts on their products. The supermarket redeems the coupon and gets the money back from the manufacturer. Meanwhile, additional sales that the retailer has obtained are partly due to the advertising on the coupon.

Other forms of coop include advertising and display materials that manufacturers provide for people who sell for them; partial payment by one business towards advertising or promotions featuring their products or services run by a second business; businesses sharing the cost of a single direct mailing by combining their advertising material; sales materials provided free or at minimal cost by one company to another; and promotional events where the cost is shared by more than one business.

Many national and regional manufacturers in various industries offer payment for cooperative advertising and promotion. You can also create opportunities to do cooperative efforts with other non-competitive businesses. This tactic can be very effective for retail and/or service businesses whose products complement each other.

Nevertheless, too few business owners take advantage of this opportunity. We often hear manufacturers complaining, 'I can't understand why they don't use the material. It's like having money in their pockets.' In essence, these suppliers are literally waiting to give retailers or service businesses money in exchange for featuring their products in advertising already planned by the business owner. The only steps required to claim that money are to enter into an agreement with the other party, then to show proof that the advertising featuring the coop material was run or broadcast as promised.

Many small business owners, both in retailing, service or manufacturing, don't fully understand the powerful benefits that coop advertising can produce for them. They look at the difficulties of fairly dividing coop print space or radio/TV time. They see the paperwork involved in reporting proof of performance and decide that coop isn't worth the effort.

In service businesses, owners are often nervous about coop, even with non-competitive businesses, because they're afraid they won't get the business — that the other coop user will get all the customers. If your ads offer benefits and your service has appeal based on a genuine consumer need or desire, that won't happen to you.

What the small business owner often doesn't see is that coop advertising can offer the coop user three business-building opportunities that no one these days can afford to refuse. They are:

(a) The opportunity to save money and/or make every pound spent on advertising buy up to 50 per cent more space or time. Also, coop can provide you with free or inexpensive display or promotional materials and other sales aids.

(b) The chance to tie in with national or other local promotions that are already building consumer awareness of products you sell, or needs that could lead customers to your services.

(c) The opportunity to build yourself a seasonal, highly liquid cashflow situation in line with your business advertising needs.

1. Pound stretchers

In today's tight-money economy, the efficient use of coop material in advertising can stretch advertising buying power by up to 150 per cent. If you use the old-style formula method of allocating 2 per cent of your projected yearly sales for advertising, using 50 per cent coop will bump that 2 per cent up to 3 per cent without your spending a penny more.

To put that into perspective, consider that 1 per cent of £500,000 is £5000. If your advertising is concentrated in your local weekly newspaper, at anywhere from 50p to £1 per line, you can buy 1000 to 5000 more lines of newspaper space with that £5000.

Even in a city newspaper at between £1 to £5 per line, that £5000 will buy you 5000 or 1000 lines you wouldn't have had on your own.

If you use the task method of budgeting for advertising, you may think that planning for coop is more difficult for you. It needn't be. Once you decide by seasons and by projected sales what you want your business to accomplish, and what your advertising and marketing objectives are, you can tie your coop advertising in with the rest of your ad campaign.

Most manufacturers you do business with are alert to the seasonal patterns and needs of your industry, and will try to fit their coop material into your peak selling and catalogue seasons. If you follow the five easy tips given in this section, you can ensure maximum cooperation from your coop suppliers or coop partners. And you still save money.

2. Tie into trends

Traditionally, independent business owners concentrate primarily on producing catalogues, leaflets, and other sales literature that can be sent by post, supplemented by some seasonal newspaper promotion.

Because of the relatively small floor space and local character of most independent businesses in the past, many retailers and service businesses have not felt the need for large-scale promotions or tie-ins with national or other local advertising, including coop.

The first and most obvious trend is that you're in direct competition for the consumer's money with department stores, discount warehouses and other mass merchandisers in retailing, and often with larger operations in service businesses. These competitors have plenty of money to spend on highly creative, hard-sell advertising that covers a larger market base than independent business owners can usually afford. Fortunately, not all competitors have mastered the basics of selling effectively in print to the consumer. But they're learning fast, and beginning to test their offers more carefully for pulling power and productivity.

To build sales in the face of this intense competition, you're going to have to be more aggressive and consumer-oriented in all of your advertising. You'll have to build higher consumer awareness of both your store or business and of the products or services you sell. That's where you can use coop advertising to your advantage.

Wherever you can, tie into manufacturers or other businesses who advertise in your region to your potential customers. Their advertising campaigns are often eye-catching, benefit-oriented, and designed to make the consumer want to buy.

By using their coop in your ad, you then take advantage of the buying mood that previous ads have already established in the consumers' minds. Also, you get the benefits of savings in both production and space costs, for advertising that helps to build your business's image.

3. Splitting the benefits
Find another service business or shop that ties in with your own, but doesn't compete so you can cross-refer customers. Then split all costs and time or space allocations right down the middle, so both advertisers get equal benefit.

Here are four examples of clever coop combinations that worked well for the advertisers involved. See if you can find another business in your community that offers you such obvious advantages:

1. A *fashion consultant and a leading clothing shop* shared an ad. The consultant even gave shows and demonstrations in the shop to guide women in selecting fashion for their life-styles.

2. An *advertising designer* and an *advertising copywriter* split their coop with an independent advertising production consultant, so that potential retail customers could be offered full-service print advertising services. All three received a fair share of business and referrals.

3. As part of a promotion, a *builders' merchant* held a draw in which a *carpenter's* services were given away free for three days to the winning customer. The retailer received more than 3000 customer names on his entry forms, and the carpenter was booked solid for a year before the contest even closed.

4. A *typist* and a local *courier service* did a promotion offering fast, efficient package deals to help local business people handle office overloads and related business

problems. The coop piece was hand delivered in selected office buildings door to door, and proved to be a real business builder for both advertisers.

Using coop advertising effectively

There are a number of elements to consider when you are incorporating coop money or materials into your own marketing plan. Here are the most important factors to be aware of in your planning.

1. Allocating space/time

One of the major problems retailers and service businesses encounter with coop advertising is determining how much print space or radio/TV time to devote to each major supplier or other local advertiser offering coop. Some product lines or services are strictly seasonal, and can be promoted only at those times when the market is obviously ready to buy them. Others can be advertised all year.

For non-seasonal, staple items, your own advertising objectives must be the guide. Do you want to build higher volume shop traffic or concentrate on higher margins per sale? Are you after a larger gift market, or do you want to position the shop to the young career and/or family women?

If your own advertising objectives are clear, you'll know exactly when to feature your nuts-and-bolts coop items and when to feature the higher-priced items. But without clear objectives, thought through months ahead, you'll probably end up in the same old 'throw in those lines quick — we're running out of time' trap that makes so much retail and business advertising a jumble of non-selling.

2. Designing a coop ad

The diagram of a retail newspaper advertising page on page 134 gives one approach to handling the allocation of coop space. Though the proportions are designed for a full page, they can be adapted both to smaller sizes of newspaper ads and, with fewer secondary features, to a catalogue page or direct mail shot.

In this example, approximately half of the real selling space is devoted to coop advertising. The headline and shop identification, though contributing to the selling effort, are really part of the shop's own positioning in the consumer's mind, rather than straight selling.

Elements of a coop newspaper advertising layout

Strong, benefit-packed umbrella headline to catch consumer attention.
Featured product or range (coop): ● large photo or drawing ● detailed tell and sell copy
5-20 other 'featured items' ● illustrated where possible
COMPLETE shop or business identification

For your coop feature, get the largest illustration you can for the space you plan to use. Studies have shown that consumers recall and react more strongly to product or service illustration than to copy alone.

In cases where you can get illustrations showing the product or service in use or installed, do so. This shows the customer more strongly what he or she will get from the product — the benefits to be received from having or using the product (see Chapter 1). Even on secondary items, use illustrations wherever you can. Ask manufacturers to help you.

2. *Back-up materials*

Back up all advertising with sales materials displayed in the office or shop, even if all you can get is a tear sheet of your ad to pin up above the featured item display or behind the reception desk.

Let your staff know what you're advertising each week or featuring in your catalogues. Make sure they're well-informed about the features and benefits or application of your advertised items or services.

Other coop opportunities

In addition to media advertising, there are other possibilities for cooperation with manufacturers or suppliers. A few are discussed below; also see the checklist on page 136.

1. Using a coop catalogue

If you produce a catalogue or product promotion leaflet, you may be able to get extra advertising revenue from the manufacturers of those products you feature. The money you receive will depend on how much space you give their products in relation to the catalogue as a whole. Major department stores coop with manufacturers in their catalogues all the time to help finance the production costs.

For your sales catalogue, ask suppliers to cooperate by giving you material that fits the type style and illustrative approach you have chosen to use.

Your printer can help set up guidelines for the manufacturer's or other business's creative department or advertising agency to follow when preparing catalogue material for you. Most manufacturers will be happy to help. After all, they want to be sure that you can use their material, because it helps build sales for them.

2. Point-of-sale materials

Point-of-sale materials are any displays or literature that help to promote the sale of a product or service where the customer buys it, whether in a shop or a business.

Coop point of sale materials are designed by manufacturers to help you sell for them in your business. Many manufacturers offer colourful point-of-sale promotional materials that you can use.

If possible, take a free-standing display unit or section of a counter display unit or section of a counter near the front of the shop or other premises and set up a display of your feature items for the week. Display in-store materials, or your own ads, near the cash register.

3. Display or offer rebated items

If you are involved in discount or rebating promotions, use the manufacturer's display materials as much as possible to feature the items on which you get coop money.

Show your staff how to build related sales on to your coop programmes. If, for example, you were featuring a line of hair dryers, put a display together with shampoos, conditioners, brushes, combs, and hair care accessories nearby.

Use your imagination to figure out what related items your staff could promote with each item you feature. Keep accurate records of sales per customer, to find out which promotions work best for your shop.

COOP MATERIALS CHECKLIST

Use the following checklist to discover what kind of coop materials are available to you for your advertising and promotion purposes.

Type of item	Supplier	Sales person	Phone
Product information	_____	_____	_____
Folders/brochures	_____	_____	_____
	_____	_____	_____
Novelty items	_____	_____	_____
Premiums or gifts	_____	_____	_____
Catalogues	_____	_____	_____
TV spots	_____	_____	_____
Radio commercials	_____	_____	_____
Newspaper blocks or ads	_____	_____	_____
Books or booklets	_____	_____	_____
Audio-visual aids	_____	_____	_____
Display cards	_____	_____	_____
Posters	_____	_____	_____
Display stands	_____	_____	_____
Labels/badges	_____	_____	_____
Demonstration films	_____	_____	_____
Sales kits	_____	_____	_____
Sample folders	_____	_____	_____
Others:	_____	_____	_____
_____	_____	_____	_____
_____	_____	_____	_____
_____	_____	_____	_____
_____	_____	_____	_____

Other coop ideas I could do:

_____

Coop record keeping with manufacturers

One frequent complaint voiced by retailers and business owners is the lack of time to keep more than the most general of records on sales and promotions. In the case of coop advertising, one objection is that it takes too much time to submit proof of performance when dealing with a number of different coop suppliers.

Yet without the time spent, the coop user cannot be properly reimbursed. And without detailed, accurate records, the user does not have a complete record of how the coop promotions work and what the customers are buying. Most coop contracts with manufacturers will require you to keep and submit those records.

If you're doing a straight 50-50 coop with another business, you won't have the proof of performance problems, but you'll still need good records on sales and effectiveness.

Coop agreements will change with each manufacturer or situation. Most such agreements will spell out exactly how much advertising you will be expected to run and how often, what proof of payment you need and your terms of payment.

You will need a system that allows you to keep track of your coop advertising by company in just minutes each week. The coop record keeping sheet shown on page 138 has been designed by the authors for retail use. It can also be used by service businesses in organising coop programmes with other businesses.

This sheet, in turn, can be coordinated with a promotion record sheet that identifies sales of featured items each week by value and by percentage of the week's sales per item.

To adapt this system for your own use, simply have a master form typed out like the one shown here. Use the long side of a standard 2-hole punched A4 sheet of unlined paper. Then take your master copy down to your local instant printer and have as many printed as you're likely to need in a year.

You can estimate that quantity by counting up the number of coop manufacturers or other businesses you plan to deal with and multiplying by 12 for the months of the year. When printed, have one of your staff fill in the information at the top of the page for each current coop supplier. This can be done at the beginning of each month. With this system, you then have all the information you need in one place. Put all your coop sheets into one binder for easy reference.

COOP ADVERTISING RECORD

Supplier: ———————— Dates covered: ———————— Product range(s): ————————

Address: ———————— Sales £ on features: ————————

Phone: ———————— Contact: ————————

Type of material	Date(s) run	Size of complete ad	% Coop	Medium name and address	Product(s) featured	Cost of entire ad	Date proofs submitted	Date paid	Amount received

In your coop binder, also put in the same number of 9 x 12 in manila envelopes with holes punched in the sides. Label each envelope by manufacturer. As your tear sheets and confirmations come in, simply place them in the envelope of the coop supplier(s) involved, along with any other records pertaining to that manufacturer's coop material.

Once you have this system in operation, you can decide how often you want to submit proof of performance. If you're using extensive materials from one manufacturer, you might want to submit your proofs once a month or more. For suppliers whose material you use less frequently, you may want to submit material every other month, or when you've collected enough proofs to make your reimbursement worthwhile.

Whatever terms you decide to use, inform the manufacturer's representative what you're doing, and make sure that your terms fit your original coop agreement with that supplier. Some manufacturers will take proofs up to six months after you have advertised. Most request them within two months.

Building cash flow

Once you have established your basic guidelines for coop reimbursement, this system can help you regulate your cash flow for your seasonal or occasional advertising needs. Before you can do this, you will probably need at least one season and possibly two, as ordinarily coop reimbursement is paid after you have completed your peak advertising seasons.

The key to making this aspect of your coop system work is in your own record keeping. On the form, be careful to fill in the date you submitted your proofs of insertion to the manufacturer and the date when you were subsequently reimbursed.

Within three months, you'll have a fairly accurate picture of the paying patterns of each coop supplier. You'll know which manufacturers take a month to pay, which ones pay within 10 days, and which take longer. This will give you another planning guide for keeping your cash flow in line with your advertising needs.

If you have set advertising objectives both by selling seasons and product lines featured, you can then finance a portion of each season's advertising with the coop money from the preceding season. By analysing the payment patterns of your suppliers, you'll know when to submit the proof on one season's advertising to get the most effective use of that money for the following season. Also, you'll have a pretty good idea of when you'll have the cash in hand to reinvest in your campaign.

Getting the best out of your coop materials

The best way to get the most out of your coop advertising is to take the time to help coop suppliers help you. Don't just find out what they have to offer. Ask for suggestions on how to use their material most effectively to fit into your objectives. Find out what's happening in other areas of retailing or service businesses. Look for market trends in your area, and share them with the manufacturer's salesperson.

Also, don't hesitate to make suggestions, and even complaints. A supplier or coop partner who doesn't know what you need can't give it to you. Don't forget that you're in business together. You both want sales. You both want repeat customers. You both want new business. Cooperative advertising can be one of the most effective ways to make sure that both of you get what you want.

Following are five easy ways to get more out of your coop materials:

1. *Let your partners know your plans.* Share the broad outlines of your marketing and promotional plans for the year with your suppliers' salespeople or your prospective coop partner. If they know what you're trying to do, they can give you more specific help.
2. *Know how your materials work.* Make sure you know exactly how each piece of material you receive is to be used. If the purpose of a piece isn't clear to you, ask.
3. *Tell suppliers or partners what doesn't work.* If you find you can't use a particular piece, don't just throw it out. Return it to the salesperson with an explanation of why you can't use it, and what other material would prove helpful.
4. *Know your customers' needs.* Make sure you know your own customers well enough to know what items they will buy and when, particularly if you are in a different type of market from the coop suppliers. The more you know, the more accurately you can choose coop material that fits your own marketing needs.
5. *Get materials to fit local media specifications.* Make sure you know what your local advertising media require in terms of production (blocks or proofs, artwork etc), then let your coop suppliers know too.

Chapter 8

Managing Your Selling Time Effectively

30 Time wasters that cost you sales

You may not immediately see how each of the following time problems can affect your business, but read on. You'll probably recognise more than one of these traits that bedevil you or your staff. Once you've spotted them, deal with them as soon as you can. When you're in business, especially for yourself, you can't afford the profit drains that these habits represent. The time you are wasting is time you could be devoting to increasing your sales.

These 30 time management areas should help you discover new ways to increase your business profits and use your own resources better. Time is one of the areas in your life over which you have the most control. Use it wisely, and you'll be rewarded with more sales, profits, and time for yourself.

1. Scattered phone calls that interrupt your day
How many times do you pick up the phone each day to discover that someone just wants to chat or hand you problems that should be taken care of by someone else? Have your secretary or assistant screen your calls as much as possible, and get the caller's message and phone number. Then you can choose a time to return all your calls at once.

Banking your calls at a set time also allows you to prepare and organise any information you need to answer the caller's questions. That saves you time on the phone, as you don't have to put the receiver down to go searching through your desk or files for the information.

2. Visitors who drop in to chat, not to buy
Socialising, in itself, doesn't make sales or get your work done. Nor do you have to 'chat up' customers or clients at length to make a sale. Certainly a few pleasant remarks or general questions are fine, but if customers or clients are there to buy,

they are more interested in what your product or service can offer them than in chitchat.

Friends or staff who are wasting time can be gently but firmly discouraged, or put off until after working hours. You can always say something like, 'I'd love to talk to you now, but I have this report for (whatever) that's due at 12, and I'm running late. Can we continue this chat when I'm done?'

3. Disorganised records, files, desk or briefcase

Disorganisation in any form is a major time waster. It can range from not being able to find what you need to close a sale, or handling the same letter more than three times, to not being prepared adequately for meetings or problems that arise.

Organisation doesn't necessarily mean neatness. As long as you know where things are that you'll need, and can put your hands on them immediately when you need them, you're organised. I know executives with neat desks who are disorganised. I also know small business owners who have piles of papers scattered all over in seeming disarray who are highly organised.

Even the neatest files or desk systems are inefficient if they don't allow you instant access to facts or presentation materials required.

If you carry a briefcase, check it each day to see that you'll have what you need for every appointment or situation you'll meet during that day, in the order you'll be using materials. Your sales presentation and closing materials should be ready to use at all times.

4. Not knowing what has to be done when

If you don't keep updated working schedules, with every step leading to your sales objectives or completion of an assignment spelled out visibly, you could miss doing what has to be done.

Schedule each project or interim sales goal back from your projected completion date. Put in every action to be done, person to contact or information you need by what date to get the work done on time.

For sales goals, work out how many people you need to see or phone each day to get the number of sales you've indicated. Then follow through every day.

5. Poor priority planning

Unless you know which tasks are most important to accomplish your business and sales objectives, you can get trapped into poor time use. Sort tasks into categories according to their contribution to productivity and meeting objectives. If you know, for example, that you should be spending 75 per cent of your time making sales calls, you won't allow yourself to get swamped in secondary administrative work.

6. Spending too much time on unimportant or unprofitable tasks

The Pareto Principle states that 80 per cent of the results will come from 20 per cent of the effort (or 80 per cent of your sales will come from 20 per cent of your customers). Knowing where to apply your efforts is one of the keys to successful business (and profit) management.

If you're too involved in routine or unimportant details, you'll miss opportunities for sales. Look at your time use patterns to see where you could be putting more time into that key 20 per cent then delegate the less profitable activities as much as possible.

7. Trying to be perfect all the time

Perfectionism can sometimes have a very high cost, usually without adequate return to justify the extra time wasted. Once you've done the very best you can in a situation, going over it again and again to try to make it perfect is taking time away from tackling new opportunities.

I'm not suggesting slipshod work here, or letting things go that are wrong for customers, clients or your business. But there will be times when you need to recognise that there is only so much you can do on a job or for a customer or client. Once you've done that, further efforts will probably be unprofitable and a misuse of your valuable time.

8. Doing it all yourself

Many entrepreneurs feel that no one can do all the things they do as well as they can. Up to a point, this can be true. Even so, once you've turned your dream into a business, you can waste a lot of time in trying to handle every detail. Train an assistant or a staff member to handle routine matters, so you're free for long-range planning, thinking, and selling.

Engage outside experts to handle areas such as accounting, bookkeeping, advertising, market development, or distribution on a freelance or contract basis. Doing it all yourself can slow down your business growth.

141

9. Communicating unclearly with customers or staff

You can waste a lot of time and people resources if your staff don't know what they are supposed to be doing. You can also lose sales if customers don't know clearly what to expect from you.

Make sure your communications are clear and complete. Double check so you know that people understand what you mean. If people ask you the same questions more than once, it means you weren't clear the first time.

10. Keeping others waiting

Lateness is rude and a time waster as well. Keeping a customer waiting can lose you a sale. Keeping staff members waiting takes them away from more profitable or productive activities.

Of course, you'll run across people who keep you waiting to show how important they are. But *you* don't need to do that. Stay well-organised and time-conscious, and you don't have to keep others idly waiting.

11. Always saying 'yes'

Some business owners take on far more than they can handle simply because they're reluctant to say 'no' to anyone. If you take on too much, you won't be able to deal with your top business priorities effectively.

When you're asked to take on a new job or volunteer work or do a favour, think through its potential impact on both your time and the rest of your workload.

12. Unrealistic time estimates

Most people tend to under-estimate the time it will take them to close a sale, complete a job, or meet business objectives. If you're keeping an accurate record of how your time is spent, it will show you how long it really does take to accomplish various tasks.

When you're giving clients or customers time/cost estimates, the accuracy of your estimates will have a lot to do with their level of satisfaction. Better to over-estimate and come in early than to be late when a customer needs your product or service.

13. Lack of planning

Too many business owners don't take the time to plan, preferably in writing, where they want their businesses to be five years from now. If you don't have an overview, or a business plan, make one. Otherwise you'll waste time on activities that don't lead to your goals or can undermine your company's profitability.

Plan each day, each week, and each month, as well as setting your yearly sales and business objectives. You need both long-range and short-range planning to stay on track and keep your competitive edge. You also need to be able to adjust regularly to new market conditions, for which you need time to plan.

14. Having too many (or not enough) meetings

Meetings can be a double-edged trap. Unless they're necessary, well-organised with a written agenda, timed rigorously, and include everyone who is essential to complete the tasks on hand, meetings can be a waste of time.

Before you schedule a meeting, see if there aren't other ways to handle the situation; that could include anything from reports to quick discussions in the office.

If you do need meetings after that, plan them carefully for optimal efficiency. Write everything out and stick to your agenda.

If staff, suppliers or clients *need* meetings, use these techniques to make them work.

15. Not getting enough information to do the job

In every selling situation or business decision area, there are certain facts that are essential to closing the sale or making a profitable decision. If you don't have those particular facts on hand and organised in selling, you'll waste time looking or going back for them, and may lose the sale.

Make sure you've considered every question the prospect is likely to ask. Cover all the answers in your presentation or your mind. Know where all your support data is, so you can pull it out quickly as it is needed.

In making business decisions, analyse the areas where you *must* have facts, then concentrate on researching those areas first in an organised fashion.

16. Needing too much information before making decisions

There is an optimal level of information you need to know that will help you make more accurate decisions. Beyond that level, it's too easy to get lost in irrelevant details.

It's also a trap to keep gathering and gathering more information as a way to avoid making decisions. Very few owners or executives have every bit of information they want and/or need for foolproof decisions. That's why so much business has an element of risk or uncertainty.

As long as you have your top priority information to give you basic boundaries, you can make reasonably well-informed decisions. No one is 100 per cent right, so why waste time avoiding decisions?

17. Good old-fashioned procrastination and its twin, indecision

Most effective owners, managers, and executives we've talked to find that when they procrastinate, they can usually trace it back to one of 10 factors:

1. Fear that they won't succeed or do well enough at that task
2. Fear that they are doing something wrong for themselves or the client
3. Insecurity about tackling new tasks or assignments outside the ordinary run of their businesses
4. Not wanting to do the task, or having been pressured into it by others
5. Disliking the person for whom they are doing the job, or with whom they have to deal to accomplish the task
6. Fear of criticism from others
7. Not feeling ready or properly prepared for the job
8. Resistance to work or personal pressures arising around that task
9. Not knowing *how* to do what has to be done
10. Not wanting to appear incompetent or less than perfect

Most of these reasons are tied into emotions that have to do with the person, not the job. Indecision works the same way, and both waste valuable selling time. The best way I know of to deal with these two is to break the task down into manageable parts and tackle it. When you're absorbed in *doing*, you're too busy to be rationalising or fearing.

18. Not finishing tasks or projects you start

Uncompleted projects can prove real time wasters. Not only do they hang over your head, often distracting you from other important tasks, they take longer to get back into once you've dropped them. Set aside specific times during your working week when you can take a task and finish it right away.

If you are handling your own preliminary bookkeeping or

sales recording and administrative functions, allot regular blocks of uninterrupted time so that you can get them out of the way completely.

19. Duplicating someone else's task
Look through your business thoroughly for signs of duplicated effort that wastes time. You don't need to be doing invoicing, filing, typing, record keeping or follow-up work if you're paying someone else to do it. The same goes for work you engage outside experts to do, such as accounting, auditing, preparing advertising, printing or whatever.

When you hire someone, it is to save you work and time — you don't need to *be* a copywriter if you can *hire* a copywriter.

20. Solving problems that aren't yours
Clients, customers, suppliers and staff will often waste your time getting you involved in solving their problems, if you let them. It's great to be able to assist people in genuine need, but too often this type of problem is caused by laziness, inefficiency or sheer thoughtlessness on the part of others.

Don't get involved. Your time as a business owner is too valuable to be given away indiscriminately. Encourage people to find their own solutions, and be firm about not doing charity work (unless you have a set covenanting or charity policy to which you adhere).

21. Not using available time-saving resources
Dictating machines, up-to-date office equipment, computers, and outside experts can save you many hours of valuable working time. Calculate the costs of your own time and resources in doing the same job without these time-savers. Then incorporate as many of them as possible into your business. They will finance themselves in the time you save, which frees you to make more money.

22. Listening too much to other people's problems
I used to have friends and even business colleagues (who should know better) calling me during the working day to discuss their business and personal problems. If you have the same time-wasters, try encouraging them to ring back after working hours. This is especially important for people with offices in their homes. Many people assume when you work at home that you're always available.

If you're in business seriously, make it clear to friends that work hours are for *work*. If you keep flexible hours, tell them when the best times are for you to talk. You can put people off without being rude about it. Remember, in business, time is one of your most precious commodities.

23. *Running from crisis to crisis*

Crisis managers usually get that way because of poor time use, inefficient people and resource allocation, disorganisation, or not staying aware of customer or market needs. If you are fire-fighting all the time, you won't have enough time to run your business for profit. Crisis management is often a function of misinformation, making mistakes that then take extra time to correct, neglecting customer needs, or unclear communications.

Spend your extra time beforehand to ensure you don't make those types of mistake, and you will not have to spend nearly as much time afterwards to correct them. Monitor your staff to catch those small inefficiencies that can lead to major crises.

24. *Not being specific enough about goals, tasks, responsibilities*

You need to be as specific as possible about every aspect of your business, and particularly your sales goals. Saying you want to 'increase sales substantially' isn't enough. General goals don't give you guidelines for how to spend your time most profitably.

However, if you know that you want to 'get a 10 per cent increase in sales of x and 20 per cent more y sold over the next six months', and you have written down how many people you need to see, or ads you need to prepare and run, to achieve those sales goals, you can allocate your time according to your tasks.

25. *Not reacting quickly enough to change*

Whether you're dealing with changes in the market place, in product technology, customer buying patterns or usage patterns, you must be prepared to react quickly to changes. Selling into new trends, clearing out obsolete products, discontinuing unprofitable services, and finding and serving new customers or clients are all part of change management — and can make big differences in your sales success.

Put aside some time each week or month devoted entirely to change management. Keep your reading in your field up to date so you know how others are handling changes. Read the trade publications in your field selectively, and have your staff bring you any newspaper cuttings or other trend information they find that show possible changes that could influence your business.

26. Not balancing workloads to priorities

You may know your priorities clearly, but if you're not balancing your time and effort accordingly, you won't accomplish them. Use the 20/80 per cent principle mentioned in 6. above to weed out your workload and realise your efforts. That way you'll end up putting your time where your profits are.

We have found that we can cut our time on a project in half by taking on specialists to help us in less profitable areas, so we can spend more of our time in writing, doing new business presentations, and thinking/consulting, which is where our profits come from. Look for your own profit priorities and restructure your time accordingly.

27. Not letting your staff do their jobs

If you recruited well for the tasks in hand, you can trust your staff to do their jobs. (If you didn't, find new people who can be trusted to perform to your standards.) Give them the authority to go with their responsibilities.

Don't waste their time (and more importantly, your own) hanging over them, answering trivial questions or handling problems your staff should be able to take care of unsupervised. Don't withhold necessary facts from staff. Provide them with everything they need to do their jobs, then let them do it. The time you save can go into getting more sales.

28. Handling written materials too often

Letters, invoices, memos and reports should be acted on as they come in. If you're not ready to handle them immediately, file them by the dates on which they can be answered, paid, or dealt with. Try not handle any written item more than twice — once when received and once to act on it.

File written materials as soon as you're done with them, so you aren't cluttering up your desk or your mind with them. Shuffling papers around again and again is not an efficient way to use time. Keep only those things you intend to deal with each day on top of your desk and file the rest.

29. Not using the people you have most effectively
Many owners don't have an accurate knowledge of staff strengths and weaknesses. As a result, staff members can often waste time and experience frustration in being given tasks at which they do not excel.

Put your people where their strengths are, and they will be more productive and motivated. Many salespeople are great at contact work with people and terrible on administrative details, so don't waste a good salesperson on paperwork. Have them dictate short call reports as they go along, then have a good secretary transcribe them. If salespeople are disorganised, get someone in to help them organise and follow through, so they can concentrate on sales.

30. Not taking enough time for thinking and
long-range planning
Outside sales and production, one of the most critical lifeblood areas of business management is planning and ideas. You need time to think. You need to think about ways to improve profitability, get more sales, set clear long-range objectives, cut costs, and improve overall business performance.

Take that time regularly, even if it means booking into a hotel for a day and brainstorming with your key people, or taking off for a weekend by yourself with no distractions.

Time/Cost management for consultants and personal service business

In consulting, writing, illustrating, the professions, accounting and bookkeeping, and most other service businesses, your time is both your stock of goods and one of your biggest cost factors. It needs careful control.

Unless you have accurate and detailed records of how and for which assignments your hours are spent, you're not in control of your business time. You also need records to show you whether the fees you get are enough to cover both your time and your overhead costs.

1. Keep a master system
Whether it's a desk book, wall calendar or time sheet, you need a complete time portrait of your business. The more specifically you can record where your time is going the better.

Calendar or diary sheets that allow you to record every 15 minutes or even 10 minutes are the best for consultation and service businesses.

2. Have a portable system with you at all times

You also need a pocket diary that helps you stay organised and record your actual time use during the day. Get into the habit of automatically recording what you're doing (and for whom) as you go along.

At first you'll be surprised how much of your time is spent unproductively. Once you've become aware of that tendency, a pocket diary can help you monitor your time more closely.

3. Keep time sheets by client and by job

You should know to the quarter-hour exactly how much time you spend working for each of your clients. Transfer your time records from your pocket diary each week (or day) on to master time sheets for each client. Include all the overhead time covered next, as well as your productive time. This is particularly critical if you're on an hourly fee basis, but even on a monthly retainer you should know if your fee covers all your time and costs.

4. Don't forget overhead time

Every account requires service and maintenance time, which isn't always directly productive, but should be covered in your fees and time estimates. Such time includes items like: travel, meetings, research, organising, writing progress reports or memos, telephone consultations, or even thinking time.

Though you can't always charge directly for these time-takers, some provision should be made for them when you're calculating your overall fee structure or time/cost estimates. Also, don't forget to include the time to produce new business presentations, especially those where you do *not* get the business to cover your costs.

5. Don't forget to cover your physical overhead

A proportion of your physical costs to do business should also be provided for in your fee structure. Rent and rates, power, staff salaries, delivery costs, office equipment, postage, telephone, office supplies, and services you have to pay for should be covered as well as your time.

6. Make sure your fees reflect your time

Calculate all your monthly costs and revenues. Then look at how much actual work you're doing for each of your clients. Is one client paying you less but getting more of your time? Is another client paying too much in relation to the volume of work and time spent?

Evaluate your monthly retainers on the basis of both hours and costs to you, to ensure that each account is profitable.

7. Make sure staff time is accounted for

Your staff time is a cost that should also be covered out of revenues in relation to the hours spent for various clients. Have them also record their time in a desk diary or log book, including their administrative time spent for you and *your* business.

8. Be clear about which expenses clients pay extra for

If you charge separately for travelling time, telephone calls, delivery services, copying, meeting time or any other services or expenses incurred for the client, be specific.

Let the clients know in your original negotiations what you expect, then document those expenses completely each month, or for each job. Don't surprise a client.

9. Keep a work flow chart where everyone can see it

A good idea is to keep a running job and schedule sheet on a wall somewhere, especially for large multi-stage jobs where there is more than one deadline to be met. You and your staff need to be able to see at a glance what you should be doing every week for each project or assignment in progress. Cross out items and deadlines only as each is met.

10. Make your estimates generous enough so you can stick to them

When you're selling your services, make your time/cost estimates slightly more than you expect to spend, to cover contingencies and delays, unexpected work or expenses.

You are always better off to come in slightly under your estimates when you charge clients, rather than over. Most clients dislike being asked to pay more than you originally led them to expect. That dislike can seriously interfere with contract renewals or repeat business for you.

Two common time traps

You can manage time, or have time manage you. The following case histories show how two common time traps work. Read them and then check the simple Time Management Analysis Worksheet at the end of this chapter to see how well you are managing *your* selling time.

1. Seeing prospects can be a time trap

John owns a small personnel recruitment firm that specialises in finding and placing top-level finance executives in business and industry. He considers it part of his job to go out to every function, luncheon, golf tournament, and event put on by his clients and associations or clubs in the industries he serves. His staff of three handle all the day-to-day interviewing, advertising and placement work, so John sees his function as a 'front-man' who keeps his company visible in the field. In that capacity, he sees literally hundreds of top executives a year who could at some point become eligible for his company's services. John discreetly passes out his business cards at every available opportunity.

What John doesn't realise is that, important as personal contact is in such a people-oriented business, it is not in itself enough to *close the sale*, which is what produces the profits. If a prospect whom John has seen out in the field *does* call to follow through on an opportunity, John himself is too often out of the office to serve that prospect. That means the call has to be handled by an unknown staff member, which often turns the prospects away. After all, it was John they saw and remembered, and John as president that they expected to serve them personally — if only to introduce them to the 'qualified staff expert' who would then do the groundwork.

John's personal visibility led prospective clients to expect personal service, which he could not fulfil and follow up. Until John started allocating regular and specific blocks of his time to serving and *closing* those top prospects himself, he was losing sales and profits. Once the prospect was closed, John could then delegate much of the detailed work involved in making placements, and still make blocks of time free *selectively* for important field contact.

You can see as many people as you like during a year, but if you're not closing enough sales from it, you're wasting time that could be more profitably spent.

2. *Know your time and profit level*

Marian was delighted when she landed a client for her public relations firm who was willing to pay the £1000 monthly retainer that she asked. Since her usual retainer for the four clients she already had was £750 a month, Marian assumed that she would be making an extra £250 a month, or £3000 a year, from the new client.

Time proved her wrong. The new client was demanding, perfectionist, indecisive, and meeting-happy, expecting at least one two-hour progress meeting every week and numerous other telephone consultations, service meetings and extra services that Marian was not properly equipped to provide.

Marian soon found that not only was she immersed in time-consuming details for the new client that weren't part of her job, she was starting to take time away from her old clients, who were her income base. Not until one of those old clients threatened to terminate her contract did Marian sit down and analyse *in writing* the impact of the new client on her business profitability.

She found that, based on her established hourly rate, her new client was actually *costing* her about £100 a month to maintain. Plus, by demanding her time at the expense of other clients, the new client threatened to cost her another £500 a month in lost business. Marian immediately resigned the new account and spent the time in serving the other clients and picking up another, less demanding new account.

TIME MANAGEMENT ANALYSIS WORKSHEET

1. Here are the five most serious time traps I fall into, and what I intend to do to get out of them:

Trap	What I plan to do	By what date
_____	_____	_____
_____	_____	_____
_____	_____	_____
_____	_____	_____
_____	_____	_____

2. Here are the three areas in which I can help my staff use their selling time more productively:

   (a)

   (b)

   (c)

3. *Time management exercise.* Keep a complete and accurate time log in 15-minute or half-hour stages, to see exactly where your time is going. Log such items as actual selling time, time spent on writing or presenting new business proposals, administrative time, time spent answering staff questions, telephone time, planning time etc. If you are already using a system such as the day-timer daily planner, analyse your actual time use patterns over the last month.

4. My real hourly wage based on the hours I spend on my business is £ _____ .

5. Areas where I could reorganise my own time for better management:

   _____

   _____

   _____

   _____

   _____

153

Chapter 9
Evaluating Your Sales Success

The sales revenue you bring in through your business is the best possible measure of your success. Whenever you see a marked increase in sales, you will want to analyse what you have been doing right, so you can do it again.

The questions and tips outlined in this chapter are designed to assist you in further analysis throughout your selling year. They should be used *in addition to* the worksheets you have completed throughout this book.

Review your plan regularly

You should use this entire book as a working manual at least once every quarter. Review Chapter 1 regularly, to make sure you are still accurate in your assessment of your product benefits. Look through Chapter 2 at least twice a year, to see if there are any new business opportunities or new customer groups you have overlooked.

Chapter 3 could be reviewed every single week, as your direct selling techniques are the heart of your sales. Chapters 4 to 7 can be used as they are needed, but should be reviewed at least once a year as a reminder. Use the whole book whenever you are doing future planning for your business.

12 Ways to evaluate your sales success

There are 12 questions you should be asking yourself each quarter. Your answers will help you evaluate whether your marketing plan and sales efforts are still appropriate for your business conditions.

The most practical way you can use these questions is to monitor your own selling success. They can serve as a basis for a quarterly marketing assessment, so you are always aware of how your business is actually working and growing.

Here are the 12 questions:

1. Are my objectives still specific and detailed? Have I spelled them out clearly for this quarter? Are those objectives attainable in my market under the business conditions I face now?

2. Am I achieving all the objectives I originally set? Are there changes in market conditions which could explain why I'm not? Have there been changes in the way I manage my business?

3. Do I still know what my customers want? Am I taking full advantage of opportunities to find out more about their needs? Do I sell to new needs that I discover?

4. Are my budget and staff allocations proving adequate to meet my objectives? Have I balanced my business resources with my marketing activities? Am I spending too much time on relatively unprofitable activities?

5. Is my entire business organised as efficiently as possible? Can I spot problems quickly? Do I have up-to-date records on jobs in hand, stock orders and deliveries, costs by product or service, and by account?

6. Have my media selection and timing proved successful? Have I found noticeable increases in business during promotional activities or features sales? Have I built in ways to monitor the results of my advertising?

7. Have I realistically segmented my market by customer group, by areas, by product demand, or however else I can? Are my advertising and promotion appealing to those groups from which my best profit opportunities would be likely to arise? Am I attracting the people who will buy the services or products I carry?

8. Have my pricing policies proved successful? Are they still competitive and in line with my business position in the market place?

9. How is my performance in the market place compared with my competition? Why am I doing better (or worse) than they are? Are my criteria for judging success or failure realistic?

10. Am I keeping adequate records of my costs and sales information? Do they tell me what I need to know for my future planning? If not, how can I improve them so that they do?

11. Is my stock well controlled and balanced in the light of my market needs and sales objectives? Any overstocked or old lines left to clear out? Has my marketing plan included them? Has loss from theft and mark-downs (if applicable) decreased in the last evaluation period? If not, why not?

12. Is my staff hiring, training, and compensation policy proving successful? Are my key people adequate for their jobs? Are there ways in which they could be employed more effectively in helping me? Are the lines for staff communication with me as good as they could be?

This book has provided the tools and techniques you need. All you have to do now is start using them and start GETTING SALES.

SALES SUCCESS ANALYSIS WORKSHEET

Use this simple worksheet yearly or quarterly to assess your progress.

1. How much did your plan cost to put into action? £ _____

2. How many people in your total market were you
   aiming to reach? _____
   How many of them actually came in to buy? _____

3. What was the average revenue, cost and profit per order?
   Revenue _____ Cost _____ Profit _____

4. How much did customers buy? _____

5. What was the total volume of sales directly attributable
   to your marketing campaign? £ _____

6. Which ads or offers worked best?

   _____

   _____

   _____

7. What will you do next time?

   _____

   _____

   _____

8. How much sales revenue and profit will you have to achieve to
   successfully meet your future business financial goals?
   £ _____ Revenue
   £ _____ Profit

Additional Sources of Information

Useful addresses

Local libraries, town halls, Chambers of Commerce and the following:

Small Firms Division Department of Industry
Ashdown House
127 Victoria Street
London SW1E 6RB
Tel: 01-212 8667
The Department of Industry has also established a number of regionally-based small firms centres.

The London and South Eastern Region
8-10 Bulstrode Street
London W1M 5DQ
Tel: 01-487 4342
Freefone: 2444

South Western Region
5th Floor
The Pithay
Bristol BS1 2NB
Tel: 0272 294546
Freefone: 2444

Northern Region
22 Newgate Shopping Centre
Newcastle upon Tyne NE1 1ZP
Tel: 0632 325353
Freefone: 2444

North West Region
320-25 Royal Exchange Bldgs
Manchester M2 7AH
Tel: 061-832 5282
Freefone: 2444
and
1 Old Hall Street
Liverpool L3 9HJ
Tel: 051-236 5756
Freefone: 2444

Yorkshire and Humberside Region
1 Park Row
City Square
Leeds LS1 5NR
Tel: 0532 445151
Freefone: 2444

East Midlands Region
48-50 Maid Marian Way
Nottingham NG1 6GF
Tel: 0602 49791
Freefone: 2444

West Midlands Region
Ladywood House
Stephenson Street
Birmingham B2 4DT
Tel: 021-643 3344
Freefone: 2444

Eastern Region
24 Brooklands Avenue
Cambridge CB2 2BU
Tel: 0223 63312
Freefone: 2444

Northern Ireland
Local Enterprise Development Unit
Lamont House
Purdy's Lane
Mewtownbreda
Belfast BT8 4AR
Tel: 0232 691031

Northern Ireland Development Agency
Maryfield
100 Belfast Road
Hollywood
County Down
and

11 Berkeley Street
London W1
Tel: 01-629 1265

Scotland
57 Bothwell Street
Glasgow G2 6TU
Tel: 041-248 6014
Freefone: 2444

Highlands and Islands Development Board
Bridge House
Bank Street
Inverness IV1 1QR
Tel: 0463 234171

The Scottish Development Agency
(Small Business Division)
102 Telford Road
Edinburgh EH4 2NP
Tel: 031-343 1911

Wales
16 St David's House
Wood Street
Cardiff CF1 1ER
Tel: 0222 396116
Freefone: 2444

The Welsh Development Agency
(Small Business Division)
Treforest Industrial Estate
Pontypridd
Mid Glamorgan CF37 5UT
Tel: 044 385 2666

Advertising Standards Authority
2-16 Torrington Place
London WC1E 7HN
Tel: 01-580 5555
The British Code of Advertising Practice is available from the ASA at a cost of £1.80 including postage and packing.

Agricultural Cooperation and Marketing Services Ltd
(advice for farmers)
Agriculture House
25 Knightsbridge
London SW1X 7NJ
Tel: 01-235 7853

Agricultural Development Advisory Service *(advice for farmers)*
Ministry of Agriculture, Fisheries and Food
Great Westminster House
Horseferry Road
London SW1P 2AE
Tel: 01-216 6311

Alliance of Small Firms & Self Employed People
42 Vine Road
East Molesey
Surrey KT8 9LF
Tel: 01-979 2293

City Business Library
Gillett House
55 Basinghall Street
London EC2V 5BX
Tel: 01-638 8215

Consumers' Association
14 Buckingham Street
London WC2N 6DS
Tel: 01-839 1222

Cooperative Development Agency
20 Albert Embankment
London SE1 7TJ
Tel: 01-211 3000

Council for Small Industries in Rural Areas (CoSIRA)
141 Castle Street
Salisbury
Wiltshire SP1 3TP
Tel: 0722 6255

Department of Trade
1 Victoria Street
London SW1H 0ET
Tel: 01-215 7877

Design Council
28 Haymarket
London SW1Y 4SU
Tel: 01-839 8000

Direct Selling Association
44 Russell Square
London WC1P 4JP
Tel: 01-580 8433

London Chamber of Commerce
and Industry
69 Cannon Street
London EC4N 5AB
Tel: 01-248 4444

Mail Order Publishers' Authority
(MOPA)
1 New Burlington Street
London W1X 1FD
Tel: 01-437 0706

The Mail Order Traders Association
of Great Britain (MOTA)
25 Castle Street
Liverpool L2 4TD
Tel: 051-227 4181

National Federation of
Self-employed and Small
Businesses Ltd
32 St Anne's Road West
Lytham St Annes
Lancashire
Tel: 0253 720911

The National Union of Small
Shopkeepers of Great Britain and
Northern Ireland
Lynch House
91 Mansfield Road
Nottingham NG1 3FN
Tel: 0602 45046

Further reading

Directories

The Top 1000 Directories Used in British Libraries
(Alan Armstrong & Associates) is worth consulting on the availability
of directories that will be useful to you.
Dun & Bradstreet publish annually *Key British Enterprises* which lists
Britain's top 20,000 companies and their directors, but costs £130.
Kompass publish the *Register of British Industry and Commerce* which
lists approximately 27,000 names, company names, mainly
manufacturers.
Kelly's Directories publish a *Manufacturers and Merchants Directory.*
Times Books Ltd offers *The Times Top 1000*, listing UK companies in
order of turnover.
Yellow Pages list telephone subscribers by trade or profession; a separate
volume is published for each area.

Other books from Kogan Page

Be Your Own PR Man, Michael Bland, 1981
Consumer Law for the Small Business, Patricia Clayton, 1983
Direct Mail: Principles and Practice, Robin Fairlie, 1979
How to Advertise, Kenneth Roman and Jane Maas, 1979
How To Be a Better Manager, Michael Armstrong, 1983
Law for the Small Business, Patricia Clayton, 3rd edition 1982
Market and Sales Forecasting, Gordon J Bolt, 1981